Born in Stockport - Grew up i

Maurice Perkins bool

A true story of life in Greater Manche: seventies that pushed a boy to become a ma... ... ...oyal Navy.

Armed Forces experiences that catapulted his development and forged bonds with comrades who became friends for life and the lessons learned that he took with him into civilian life.

The story is told in a humorous and gritty style, describing events and incidents, fast paced and straight from the heart. Mostly funny, there is a sober and occasional sad side to the events, which match the ups and downs of life.

Maurice describes himself as a Scallywag who became an Executive. Never slow in expressing himself, he paints a picture of life that is not always visible to everyone.

Preface

Conversation, verbal exchanges, providing and responding to oral instructions are all a daily part of life and something I have always enjoyed. Having a laugh when I can, ensuring that people understand or that I understand what is needed and what is going on. However, it has been noted, many, many times, by many people, that I can be a bit lippy.......

So, what does being a bit lippy mean. Seeing the funny side of things when others cannot but speaking out anyway, ad-libs, swift responses, that sort of thing. I can quip with the best and am easily disappointed with the opposite, which I call "slopes" or slow responses. Where someone has to really think to say something remotely witty. Me, I can throw them off the cuff with the best of people.

However, quips have got me into lots of different types of trouble over the years, including having my head kicked in (literally), falling out with friends and family, resorting to fisticuffs (many times) or reducing a sombre business gathering into fits of laughter. I like to make people laugh.

All of these accounts are based on real events, involving real people and recollected from my perspectives. No harm is intended, other than to inform our social history and make people smile. I hope you enjoy the read...

Maurice Perkins

aka Moz, aka Polly, aka Mo

Born in Stockport - Grew up in the Royal Navy

Book One of Two

Glossary of Terms

AB	Able Rate / Able Seaman
Bobbins	Rubbish
Bootneck, or Bootie	Royal Marine
Crabfat	Airman
Dabtoe	Seaman
Dhoby	Wash or Clean
Fag	Cigarette
Gash	Rubbish
Gopher	Big Wave
Guzz	Plymouth
Hank Marvin, or just Hank	Starving (hungry)
HMS	Her Majesties Ship
Hooky	Leading Rate / Leading Hand
Joss	Master At Arms, chief of naval police
Matelot	Sailor
Mither	Continually harangue
NAAFI	Navy Army Air Force Institute
Oggin	The Sea
Oppo	Close friend, mate, opposite number
Pompey	Portsmouth
Pongo	Soldier
POTS	Petty Officer Telegraphist
RA	Ration Allowance (for staying in civilian accommodation)
RS	Radio Supervisor (Petty Officer)
Scablifter	Naval medic
Scallywag	Street urchin, trouble causer, thug
Slate	Amount of debt owed
The mob	HM Armed Forces
Vet	Naval medic
WAFU	Fleet Air Arm – Wet And Fucking Useless
Zed's	Sleep zzzzzz

Born in Stockport - Grew up in the Royal Navy

Opening chapter

Commanders Table

Six of us line up as defaulters. All able and ordinary seamen Radio Operators. Arrested the night before we sailed after getting into a fight with sailors off another ship. To ensure that we didn't get our stories mixed up we had elected our divisional officer, Lieutenant Leonard to represent us, after briefing him of the actual details of the fight.

We had been drinking all evening in the NAAFI club in HMS Cochrane and were making our way down the road to the Rosyth dockyard gates, only a few hundred yards down the road, with the usual posse of Ministry Of Defence Police manning the gate waiting for us.

We strolled down laughing and giggling at all the funny stuff that had been going on that evening including the drinking competition and some of the jokes that we still remembered in our inebriated state. A black cab pulled up and four lads climbed out in our path. Well three of them climbed out on the pavement side and we heard a mighty thump as the fourth guy fell out backwards hitting his head on the tarmac.

Concerned, we offered to help the unfortunate lad up but his mates pushed us away said they could sort it themselves. I can remember that the guy on his back looked very tall, as big as me and his legs were still in the taxi. Someone started to laugh at the funny predicament, of him lay on his back in the road and his feet in the cab and wandered off towards the dockyard gate.

As we toddled along laughing there was a commotion behind us and we stopped to see what it was. Coming towards us was this massive lad who had to be 6' 6" at least and powerfully built, throwing slow air punches and demanding that we stop laughing and face up to his Geordie pride, with his three mates making similar noises behind him.

We kept laughing and turned to the dockyard but one of our oppo's Billy Lounton, a gritty Geordie himself, turned round to placate the giant and probably say something funny. However, he unfortunately walked into one of the big lazy haymakers thrown by the big guy and went down like a sack of shit.

This brought an instant response from the five us still standing and we launched an assault on all four of them. Punching and kicking them until only the big guy was still standing. Stevie Yorke launched a kick at him and I went in with a sort of rugby tackle and down he went.

A very bloodied Billy decided to re-enter the fray and promptly sat on the big guys chest and started punching him in the face. In that moment, probably to keep honours even, everyone sort of stopped whilst Billy got his own back with a couple of punches. But the big feller rose in a Frankenstein sort of movement, slowly sitting up until he was face to face with Billy who was still throwing punches.

The big guy then pawed him with one of his meaty hands and Billy went down again. The big feller didn't exactly punch him straight to the face, he sort of slapped Billy with his big fists, once, twice and blood was exploding everywhere. Without any words I kicked the giant in the side of the head and Stevie kicked him in his side. We did this two, or three times, until he went down again. Then after some further scuffling, both groups parted. They to tend the giant and us to drag Billy back to our ship.

The MOD Plods were beckoning us in towards the gates, having not had a proper view, they were telling us to avoid all that trouble over there and get back to our ships safely. Then they saw the state of us. Blood everywhere, torn clothing and the barely conscious Billy strung between two of us and bleeding from his mouth, nose and a big cut over one eye. Then it was all whistles and out truncheons as the other boys and us began jostling again in the narrow gap of dockyard gates.

They arrested us and called in the Royal Navy Regulators, who arrived within seconds and took all ten of us to cells for the night and a series of interviews and physical examinations. We were only let go when the Regulators had got all the information they needed and escorted us back to our ships for booking in there.

Once Billy got cleaned up and passed fit for his bunk, we could get below and pick up some much needed Zed's...

Next morning was the walk of shame as the broadcast "Call The Hands" at 06:45 was followed shortly after by another pipe naming all six radio operators and the order to report to the ships senior police officer, The Master at Arms.

Stand to attention. Receive the charge. Instructed to appear at Officer of the Days table for defaulters at 16:30.

The older guys knowing the craic would not make a plea at Officer of the Days table later that day as they knew that he didn't carry the rank to deal with the charges of Drunk & Fighting Ashore. A serious breach of the Naval Discipline Act.

No plea meant no explanation that could limit our ability to manoeuvre out of too much trouble as those words under caution would be used against us at the next level. The Commanders Table.

We elected our Signals Communication Officer, SCO Lieutenant Leonard to defend us and had briefed him on the exact circumstances, or as close to it as we could, that we had been attacked and were defending ourselves. We did this as under questioning, one of us could slip up and leave us all exposed to the Commanders wrath if our stories conflicted or got mixed up in the intensity of questioning.

All seemed to be going well enough in the exchange between Lt. Leonard and The Commander and he seemed satisfied that we had acquitted ourselves quite well in our defence. When he asked what seemed to be an innocuous question of how long we had kicked the big guy in the head to get him off RO William Lounton? Two or three kicks, less than ten seconds but the SCO looked down at his notes and read the description of the entire fight, which had lasted no more than 3 minutes.

The SCO looked up and said "Three minutes" whilst we had to remain motionless, silent and shocked as the Commander shouted "THREE MINUTES, you kicked a defenceless man in the head for THREE MINUTES!"

Which is an understandable reaction. The big guy would have died if we had kicked him in the head for 3 minutes. The Commander was incensed. The SCO shut his notebook as he had finished giving evidence and we remained at attention with our caps off whilst the Commander ranted at us about uncontrolled violence and death of comrades in arms, bringing his ship and Navy into disrepute and a whole load of other stuff. A proper tirade. Painfully received as this was rapidly becoming an injustice and more so when he issued the punishment. Seven days number 9 punishment followed by an additional seven days stoppage of leave.

Five hours extra work a day, in between normal daily watches for seven days, scrubbing dirty pans in the galley or painting someone else's part of ship and no shore leave, plus another seven days of no shore leave and no alcohol allowed. Outstanding.

Onwards and upwards then....

Chapter Two

The Royal Navy

I had joined the Royal Navy on 3rd December 1974. Signing on the dotted line and swearing allegiance to The Queen and country at HMS Ganges, Shotley Gate, near Ipswich in Suffolk. I became a "6-week wonder" as the old salts would describe us, before moving on to which ever professional branch we were in for. In my case I wanted to be a Radio Operator.

Despite my constant hunger and need to eat during the 1970's, the RN documents demonstrated that I was 5' 7½ " tall and weighed 9 stone and 6lbs on the day I became a member of Her Majesties Armed Forces. A pretty trim youth all in all.

That first day and first few weeks are a complete shock to the system. No words to really describe the moment when you swear allegiance to The Queen. It is a momentous thing but the gravity of it was lost on the wide-eyed 17-year old that I was. It was only after I left the navy did I really understand the commitment I had made. I was street wise for sure and had a little understanding of discipline and the Navy from my time with the Sea Cadets but in reality I had not got a scooby doo (clue) what I had let myself in for.

Lots of shouting, lots of double time marching from one place to another. The first 3 days of kit issue, medicals, haircuts and training. How to iron, how to wash, shave and shower. How to fold your kit up. How to stow your kit. How to clean, polish and mend. Some things made perfect sense, some things I already knew, a lot I didn't. How to march, how to walk and how to run.

I already shaved, I had big sideburns and long hair, neither of which survived the first encounter with the Navy barber. How would you like your hair sir, long on the top, save the "sidies" and feather in the rest. Of course sir, as the electric razor removed any vestige of civilian looks in a series of "BRRPP, BRRPP'Ss". Next lad. How would you like your hair sir, "BRRPPP, BRRRPPPPP".... The first bit of forces dark humour and I loved it. Hilarious once you got your head round it. Or in this case, their electric clippers round our heads. Ha ha.

The Petty Officer we were assigned to as our senior trainer, was a great old salt with the surname of Garvey and he appointed me as Deputy Class Leader, then made up to acting Class Leader for the whole 6 weeks of basic training when the designated Class Leader had a crisis of confidence until his family turned up for our passing out parade. Then he led our class through our final Divisions at Ganges. However, I led the class through the six weeks of basic training.

The basic premise of a Class Leader is to take a bit of responsibility for a body of men when out and around the camp, along with managing the mess rosters for cleaning and such like. He liked my attitude and why he made me up.

The passing out parade on our last day, was a grand affair with a Royal Marine band playing as we carried out Divisions to a variety of catchy military marching tunes. My favourite being Heart of Oak. Proper Navy marching song that one. Though once you get out of training, marching is limited to formal affairs only, plus appearances at the table when you are marched in and out for disciplinary events but more of that later...

When I got on the train at Stockport railway station on 3rd December for the haul down to London, across London on the Tube and a train out to Ipswich I was nervous as hell. My Dad was with me and gave me a kiss on the platform and pointed at some lads in the train compartment that was next to where we got on. He said you won't be alone I bet those lads are joining up and I remember looking at him and thinking really. Dad carried my bag on with me and introduced me to 3 lads from all round Greater Manchester who indeed were on their way to Ipswich as well. Fuck me, Dad was right.

One of the lads was Pete McDonnell. A huge lad. We hit it off as mates and did everything together through that first 6 weeks. We were both in the Admin block, sat at adjacent tables having what might be construed to be an HR interview today by some lovely Wren Writers. They wanted to know as much about our backgrounds as possible. Pete had quite a broad Derbyshire accent and hailed from a little village called Charlesworth. Not that far from Stockport.

Wren: "So Pete, do you play any sport?"

Pete: "Yes, I play rugby"

Wren: "Who have you played for?"

Pete: very proudly says "Charlesworth"

Wren: "Where's that?"

Pete: "Its near to Glossop"

Wren: "Where's that then?"

Pete: "Derbyshire"

And that is what she must have written because that evening after rounds, two guys in white t-shirts were jogging on the spot talking to us (Physical Training Instructors can never keep still) so where is the County Colt they wanted to know?

Despite Pete explaining that he played for Charlesworth and not the County, they took one look at his size and demanded he went with them. So they jogged off to some rugby training session in one of the gyms and Pete never looked back. While we were there he played with the ships company representing Ganges and later played for Portsmouth Command as well as Collingwood where he did his electrical training.

Basic training involves weapons handling and I loved it. I was a good shot and missed out on a marksman's badge by one hit. We had to complete the assault course oodles of times, as a team and as an individual against an average time, based on age and weight. The swimming test was a combination of strength and stamina. Fully dressed in overalls (cannot get them off) and boots. You jump into the pool from the highest diving board, remove your boots after surfacing but were allowed to place them on the side otherwise they would plummet to the deepest depths and be a struggle to get back out. Swim round the pool for a distance of half a mile or so and then climb into an inflatable raft. It was hard. Some never made it. Fail the swimming test then and you were out of the door. When you got to sea I was amazed to find the number of people who had apparently passed the test but couldn't swim. Go figure that, I certainly couldn't. Not the strongest swimmer, I used to take a deep breath and swim underwater and loved it, probably why I enjoy snorkelling so much on holidays.

The relationship with Iran at the time had led to the Royal Navy providing training for hundreds of Iranians who on average, were a lot older than us, adults in all honesty, whilst we were mainly teenagers. There was a lot of tension and quite a few fights between the Brits and the Iranians. Some took place in the big gymnasiums as organised events, whilst others were in the dark round the bowling alley and messes. All of them full on fighting. Those who got caught got into quite serious trouble as I recall.

Ganges had a bowling alley when I went there. Lots of bright lights and music, plus the banging of balls down lanes and hitting skittles. I had never been in a bowling alley and got to grips with it quite well. We had to book our lanes in advance, no chance of just turning up to play as there were so many trainees and ships company who wanted to use it. I liked to go just to hear the music and have a beer, as it wasn't a problem getting served as long as there was no trouble inside the place.

The first time I went in there, the impact of the noise and the lights combined with the record that just started to play, which was Bachman Turner Overdrive and "You Ain't Seen Nothing Yet" blasting out, that whenever I hear that song, I am taken straight back to that moment at Ganges. Without fail.

After the first 2 weeks we got 3 weeks Christmas Leave, which was a bit bizarre. Anyway, I went home on a free travel warrant and had a ball. I spent most of my holiday pay in the first week at home and had to lower the tone of my socialising.

I also went into my local Lipton's supermarket to say hello to friends I used to work with and catch up with them on things. Allport, the manager of the butcher's section, had recruited my replacement, a lad called Danny Massey but he had gone home sick and wasn't expected back until the New Year.

Allport was whinging about how much work he had on with the festive demand and asked me if I wanted a bit of casual labour. I thought "beer tokens" and said okay. We negotiated a cash rate, to be paid at the end of each day and I worked 3 or 4 days with him, Christmas Eve and a few days between Boxing Day and New Year's Day. Then it was back down to Ganges.

Straight back into weapons handling and marching. Lots of marching. Slow marching, double time, all of it. The parade ground was a busy old place with different classes marching around and making sure to avoid any directional clashes. Testing of Anti Gas Respirators (AGR's) wasn't fun. Shoved into a windowless room full of CS gas. On the day of the test after practicing a few times, you had to remove you mask inside the gas filled room and shout out your name and official number, then pause to receive the command to leave, just as you breathed in. Brilliant. Cue a bunch of coughing and spluttering trainees rolling around on the grass outside.

We had to double time all around the training camp. No walking during class hours, which ranged from as early as 06:00 and as late as 20:00, depending on what the events were. Free time in the evening was either spent in the bowling alley if we had any cash or we would take over the gym halls and create massive links of gym equipment and then play a game of "Pirates" sort of a cross between "Tick" and "British Bulldog" as once caught, you were thrown to the ground (gym floor was made out to be the sea) and then became a pirate chasing the rest of the sailors up and over the kit. It was amazing that no-one got hurt because people were thrown off the ropes, kicked down the climbing frames and tripped up navigating a line of horse boxes... That game was only surpassed by Murder Ball, a sort of medieval tennis.

The gym hall would be separated by a line of horse boxes with a pile of medicine balls lay along the top. Two sides lined up at each end of the gym. The winner was the team with the least number of medicine balls on its side of the court.

Then there was damage control and fire-fighting. The two things that will kill any ship for sure is big holes in the hull or a fire. So began the training that becomes a daily occurrence at sea. A fire and or damage control exercise to test and retest a matelot's ability to help keep a ship in the fight. Every ship, every day, is exercised and has its mettle tested, without fail.

Fighting fires is a delicate matter and use too much water and the weight it will cause a ship to list, fall over and sink. Fires are fought on six sides. The ceiling (deckhead), the four walls (bulkheads) and the floor (deck). Metal has to be cooled quickly, or heat will transfer to another compartment and so on.

The damage control exercise was a lot of drills on how to open and place a splinter box. How best to jack and stay beams and boards to prevent the inrush of water on a real ships compartment. How to maintain ships integrity and the citadel in terms of Nuclear Biological Chemical Defence and add rubber boots and gloves to your disposable green outfit to further protect you.

We seemed to master all the individual skills and then came the test. A once-only event, no repeats, no get-outs, you had to do it first time and stand on your result.

On the day of the test we double marched to an imposing looking building that had oodles of large diameter pipes heading into it from a pump house next door and more piping heading into the estuary where the rivers Stour and Orwell met at the gateway to the English Channel and the North Sea. A battery of instructors briefed us on the layout of the sealed "compartment" and showed us the holes that would be letting in the freezing cold water pumped in from the estuary to create the life-like scene of a rapidly flooding compartment.

Care was taken to explain that in a real event, the priority was always to block the biggest hole or holes first to lower the volume (and therefore weight) of the water rushing in. Then moving through all the holes until the last smaller holes, which would most probably be caused by shrapnel.

However, and this was a big however, as the Navy had to pump in the water under pressure, we had to plug the little holes first and then move onto the bigger ones. This would be the only time that this rule would be in force and it was stressed over and over again. Another one of those little physics rules about small holes and increasing water pressure. The instructors even let us lay out the kit we needed in little groups. A spar here, some bungs there and the hammers all within easy reach.

We broke down into two teams. One in first, then the other. My team was selected to go first and we formed up outside the main hatch door. A thunder flash was chucked into the compartment and the instruction to enter was screamed at us as soon as the boom was heard. Cue pandemonium.

The scene awaiting us was not the one we expected. Smoke from the thunder flash was one thing but the freezing water gushing in from all the pipes caught your breath and more crucially, had washed away all the bungs and hammers into the waters that were now beginning to rise at a rapid rate. No instructors inside, just us.

Our plan was to put one of the smallest lads onto big Jim's shoulders to attack the small rips and tears in the pipes above our heads and smack bungs in, whilst the rest of us tackled the big holes. Unfortunately, it took the pair of them some time to find the bungs and hammer. We had completed the block on the main hole as the first bung was hammered into the pipe from the shoulder mounted platform (Jim). The water pressure must have been nearest its highest because the bung shot out and hit the lad square on the forehead and knocked him out.

We lost Jim to holding him afloat whilst we had to undo the big hole cover and spar, carry out the exercise of filling the small holes, then replace the splinter boxes and big hole cover. The delay cost us a success and the water reached the level of a red line painted around the compartment. Shit. We then had to stand in the freezing cold and nearly chin height water whilst it was pumped back into tanks or back into the river, I am not sure. I do know that we got bloody cold standing there.

Once the water level subsided below that of the hatch, we could step out. Were formed into a small unit and double timed it back to the mess for a hot shower and wait for the second half of the class to carry out their test.

A feature of the early weeks was a combination of instructors rousing us at odd hours of the night or in the early hours of the morning for snap mess evacuations, or dress into a particular outfits, or for a run round the parade ground. We also had to endure mess raids from other classes, who mimicked the instructors to get a response or just turn into a fight with water hoses and using wet towels as clubs. You had to stay on your toes.

Our mess sometimes utilised a group to stay awake until the early hours as a sort of sentry guard, immediate response group and it quickly turned into a 3-card brag event to while away the hours. Gambling in the Navy is a big no no. The quickest way to create enmity is to generate debts between sailors. We did get caught twice and I got a verbal warning for it.

It is amazing that any of us passed out but we did. This is our class photograph taken the moment we were all issued with our No.1 uniforms. Some of the kids in this photo did not go on to survive their professional training but did quality to leave basic. It was winter and we had to wear the old wool pullover tops, also known as "woolly pullies" instead of cotton white fronts. A nightmare of itching and scratching. They were warm but bloody uncomfortable.

The coarse wool, woolly pullies were replaced by a much smarter version in 1976 that matched the green of the army and the grey of the flyboys, with matching elbow and shoulder patches, all in navy blue.

On completion of training, we were drafted straight to our professional training establishments and we met up with lads from other courses and had to travel in rig from Ganges into London, across the tube and onto a train down to the radio school near to Petersfield in Hampshire.

However, before that I should dip back in time and explain how I got to where I was.....

Chapter Three

Scallywag to Executive

Born into a loving family with hardworking parents, I spent all my early years living in council houses and my teens on a tough neighbourhood estate until my Dad decided to buy his council house under Tory rule, then sell and move us out.

Mum and Dad instilled values of love, creativity and respect for others property into us and they are principles that have remained with me a lifetime and have hopefully cascaded into my children and grandchildren.

However, as a teenager I was a typical scallywag in the late 60's and throughout the 70's and though only arrested once before I joined the Royal Navy, there were numerous incidents and events that I will try and describe as I outline my development. I must have had something going for me, because despite leaving school with no formal qualifications I led and won a £2.1bn Integrated Highways Contract for Skanska in the year before I retired.

But we have to start somewhere, so here we go.

Chapter Four

Reddish

Until I was about 3 years old, we lived in South Reddish, an area known colloquially as "Newtown" made up of back to back terraced houses that fronted straight onto the street. No gardens, just a back yard with a lavatory in it. No bathroom, it was tin bath (or plastic in the case of toddlers) and stand up all-over washes. Newtown was demolished in the big slum clearance programmes of the 1960's and 1970's.

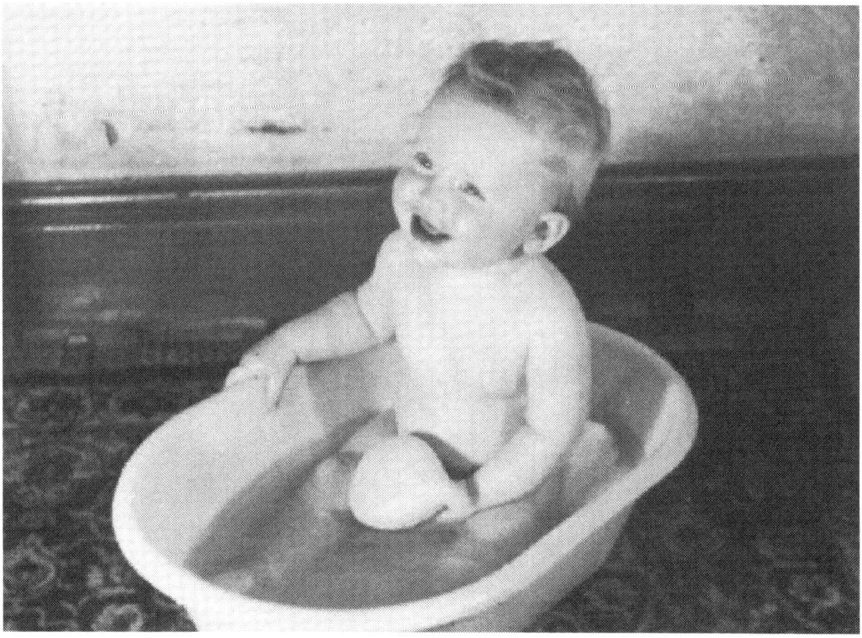

In 1960, we moved to Edale Avenue in North Reddish. My Dad said it was the coldest house he had ever lived in. During the winter of 1963, my brother David and I went to bed in pyjamas, football socks, mittens, dressing gowns and knitted bobble hats on!

We used to scrape the ice off the inside of the metal framed windows, to look outside and see how much more it had snowed overnight. Dad fitted a "heater-lamp" in the bathroom, a twin 500-watt pair of lamps in a plastic housing . It provided light like a bright sunny day and a level of heating that actually made bath nights in the winter tolerable.

The heater-lamp didn't get past 2-years old when my brother and I worked out that flicking drops of freezing cold water from the tap in the sink, made the lamp "sizzle". Great game until we threw too much water up and both lamps shattered with a bang. Sorry Dad, we don't know how it happened. We got water in our eyes and flicked our heads. It must have gone straight onto the bulbs...... as Dad carefully picked us out from all the broken bits of lamp. Honest.

Other than that, we had one open fireplace in the living room. No other form of heating in the house. I cannot remember how old I was when Dad allowed me to help him build the fire for the first time. Shovel out the cinders and ash from last night's fire that had burnt out. Sweep up as much dust and clean the grate. Twist several sheets of newspaper and lay them down on the grate. Place a few pieces of kindling in opposite direction, place a couple of pieces of coal strategically balanced on the wood. Then my Dad lit it. The fire was fed all day until we went to bed in the winter. In the summer, it was needed to heat the back boiler for hot water but only in the evenings.

At some point Dad decided I was trusted enough to light the fire.... The routine was to light a taper, get the twisted newspapers lit first. Gently blow on the flames to help the kindling light. Monitor closely until the coal got going. Add coal lumps as required. Do not stir (stoke) the fire as it burned off the coal too quickly. The idea was to generate a level of warmth in the fridge.

If the wood or coal wasn't taking, my Dad would place a sheet of newspaper over the hole to the fireplace and "draw" air into the fire, making it burn better. Lots of care had to be taken as the sheet of newspaper could instantly catch fire. Never a job for a child.

I used to play with my little soldiers and tanks on the lino (linoleum or vinyl lay) at the edge of carpet. No fully-fitted carpets in those days. The soldiers stood up better on the lino but it was always colder at the walls away from the fireplace. Too warm to play on the fireplace. Sort of a happy medium to be cold but play okay.

Dad was a lorry driver working for small family haulage firm in Reddish owned by Harry Warburton who had a big house with a small holding behind it on Sandy Lane. Dad brought all sorts of things home with him on his travels. Dumped bikes that he would fix up with bits off other bikes he had found and sell them. Once he came home with a dog he had rescued and was taking it to the dogs home but spotted Mum, my little brother David and me waiting at a bus stop fresh from having our hair cut at Fred's, the barber on Sandy Lane.

David spotted the greasy thing in a sack in the footwell and shouted that it was a rat and Dad corrected him and said it was a dog and before anyone could blink, David thanked Dad for buying us a dog. He didn't want to spoil the moment, so the dog came home with us. We called it Dino, after the pet baby dinosaur from The Flintstones but after washing the dog that night when he got home, Dad told us the dog wasn't a boy so it couldn't have a boy's name. Secretly I don't think he fancied shouting "Dino" and after a short discussion named the dog Lassie after the very popular TV series.

Another time, Dad brought home a big pile of planks that were being thrown out of a mill, or maybe they just fell off the mill onto the back of his lorry and then fell off the back of his lorry at our house, it was never really clear. All I know is that we had a load of planks stacked up in the shed, which we used like giant building blocks. Mum made us a Viking ship one day, by lining the planks up around one of the washing line poles and tied the line down to the grass with pegs, then got some material for a "sail" and helped us make swords with cardboard guards on them.

All my mates loved to come round to our house because we had a big garden for one and a Mum who loved to engage with us and help to create "adventures" and she was good at it as she had an amazing imagination that inspired both David and me.

Mum was a machinist who worked from home making shirts for Tootal and always had loads of material at hand. She made us all bandages and slings one day and added red lipstick for blood and we walked round the streets like we had just come from a disaster.

She made us a simple tent another time and did the same for my children many years later. She also made us both cowboy outfits and cavalry suits. One of the cowboy suits has been worn by 3 generations of our family. She made army outfits for my 3 children in the 90'S out of some camouflage material she bought off the market.

My best friend in those days was David Gibson. We did everything together. He always wanted to play football. I always wanted to play war.

After a number of disagreements, we settled on a compromise. Football one day, war the next. That sort of thing. Football was just thumping the ball round our back garden (cos it was bigger than his) or on the streets outside. Occasionally we would get down to North Reddish Park on Gorton Road.

We joined the cubs together, we played football for Frank Aspinall – a complete legend of a man who ran a load of different football teams on a shoestring. Frank gave me an old pair of football boots to play in my first game. Proper old fashioned cloggers with leather studs screwed into the sole. The kit was green and white stripes, white shorts and green socks. The white was more grey than brilliant but it didn't smell too much and I played my first proper game of football on the park pitch at Gorton Road, then later in South Reddish on Houldsworth Park . I hadn't got a clue. Kick and run. Kick the ball. Kick the other players. Run around chasing the ball. Ha ha.

Cycling was our mutual ground and David and I cycled everywhere. Mum and Dad would have had kittens if they knew where we went as kids. Gorton Market, Denton, Hyde, Levenshulme and all over.

Cubs was another thing we both got into. Two evenings a week. Playing old-fashioned games, boxing, camping etc. it was all great fun.

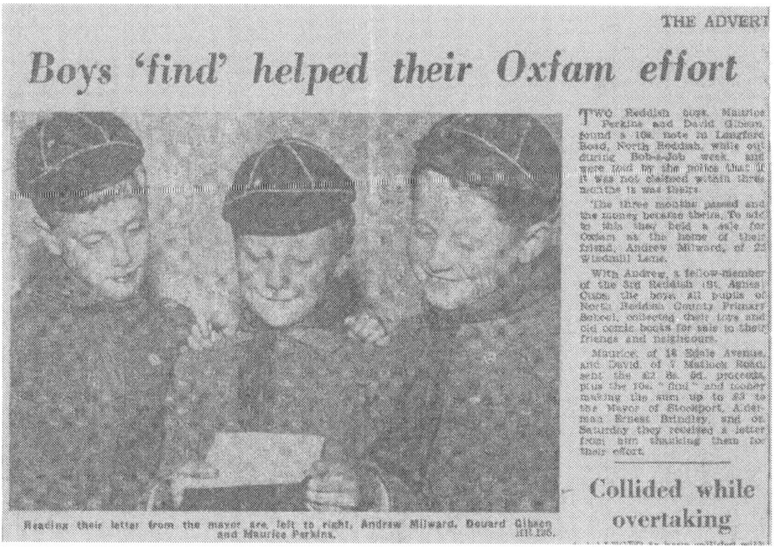

THE ADVERT

Boys 'find' helped their Oxfam effort

TWO Reddish boys, Maurice Perkins and David Gibson, found a 10s. note in Langford Road, North Reddish, while out during Bob-a-Job week, and were told by the police that if it was not claimed within three months it was theirs.

The three months passed and the money became theirs. To add to this they held a sale for Oxfam at the home of their friend, Andrew Milward, of 23 Windmill Lane.

With Andrew, a fellow-member of the 3rd Reddish (St. Agnes) Cubs, the boys, all pupils of North Reddish County Primary School, collected their toys and old comic books for sale to their friends and neighbours.

Maurice, of 14 [illegible] Avenue, and David of 7 Matlock Road, sent the £2 8s. 6d. proceeds, plus the 10s. "find" and money making the sum up to £3 to the Mayor of Stockport, Alderman Ernest Brindley, and on Saturday they received a letter from him thanking them for their effort.

Reading their letter from the mayor are, left to right, Andrew Milward, Douard Gibson and Maurice Perkins.

Collided while overtaking

Our annual fund raiser in the day, was "Bob-a-job" week. Brushing up garden leaves, cleaning cars, moving rubbish etc. our clients would give us a shilling (a bob) and we had to collect so much on a card and then hand it in to our Akela.

Whilst carrying out our efforts, we found a 10-shilling note and being good cubs, we took it to the police station on Gorton Road, Reddish and a kindly copper completed a record in his book. He told us that if no-one claimed it, we could have it.

Thoughts of bags of gob-stoppers, liquorice and lollies must have filled out heads but we had parental guidance from beings with higher principles and so with another mate, Andrew Millward, held a sale of our comic books and board games to raise money for Oxfam. Mum orchestrated a letter to the Mayor and we got one back and our picture was in one of the local rags, the Stockport Advertiser.....

They managed to spell David as Douard in the write up, which became a great source of humour as I would wind him up shouting "Come on Douard!" and he would get proper angry with me. Ha ha.

None of us had a telephone in the 60's and kids called round for each other. Our back gardens were all connected but fenced off. Sometimes I would run up Edale Avenue and round into Matlock Road to call for him. Other times I just stood at the bottom of our garden yelling "GIBBO!!" at the top of my voice until he came out and answered me. We then used to have a shouted conversation of what we were doing and where we were going.

One Saturday morning I must have decided it was a shout and not a call for and therefore stood in the corner of our garden shouting "GIBBO!" for ages without any response. When a bedroom window opposite and down the road near his house, flew open and a very angry bloke shouted "They have gone on fucking holiday you dick and I am on nights, now fuck off!" .... So I did.

We went to North Reddish primary school and then onto the juniors. I had a lot of fun there. We used to gather into two big gangs in the playground then run at each other and try and throw our opposite numbers onto the floor, girls and boys. Once you were down, you were supposed to stay down. The gang would then run over them to the other side of the playground. Turn round and repeat the exercise until one side was the winner. The teachers and dinner-ladies hated it and used to bollock us something rotten but we only halted things temporarily, then start again the next day.

Dinner times were a challenge. 8 kids randomly placed at a table. Food sloshed onto plates. Simple rules. No-one could have pudding until all 8 plates were clean. No-one could leave the table until all 8 pudding plates were clean. We had all sorts of routines. Who liked what and who didn't like what else. We would swap food, scraping stuff off and onto each others plates, then scoff. Clean dinner plates means onto pudding. Same again, swap and scrape. Eat like mad. Clean plates. Then get the okay from the dinner ladies for all 8 of us to rush out into the playground.

One particular day, none of the 7 kids I had randomly been drawn with liked the dinner main course, cheese and onion pie. I absolutely loved them. So I ate all 8 portions of cheese and onion pie. Everyone else sorted out the spuds and greens. Great stuff. Puddings didn't seem to be a problem, so they all got seen off and out we went.

After running around like a demented idiot for about fifteen minutes, I felt a bit funny. Then I felt sick. I managed to make it back to the school building and a dinner lady escorted me into the bathroom where I promptly threw up about 8 portions of cheese and onion pie in a series of explosions..... Never really been able to eat cheese and onion pies to this day for some reason ....

When we used to go cycling, sometimes it was mob handed. Alan Kniverton, Andy Moores, Robert Wilkins, David Gibson, Nipper Johnson and Andrew Brittain. We were all due to meet at Nipper's house one Saturday lunchtime and David, Nipper and me were in his living room waiting for others when his big sister and her mates came in. They were all teenagers, bear in mind we were 8 or 9 years old and they were "going out" whether that was the matinee at the Essoldo cinema on Gorton Road or shopping downtown, I don't know. What I do know is, one of them decided to practice kissing on the 3 of us....

I have to say, 4 or 5 big girls squeezing us so we couldn't run away and smothering us with French kisses was a massive turn-on when I had no idea of why I felt so excited by it all. Brilliant. They thought it was really funny and kept egging each other on with shouts of encouragement, whilst we squirmed. We couldn't wait to get away, onto our bikes and leg it.

It was only afterwards when I was trying to work out what the sensations were, did I make any sense of it. Who doesn't like a bit of female domination? Anyway, moving on...

There were a number of corner shops in those days, half of someone's house converted into a shop front and sold stuff. The one outside the school gates was a sweetshop. Excellent commercial location to tap into the sweet teeth of small children. The lady who ran the place had trays already set up for the kids.

The cheapest was probably the farthing tray, although the coin had been phased out a year or so before, still had a trade of four sweets per penny (the same value as a farthing, one quarter of a penny). Then there was the ha'penny tray (two for a penny), the penny tray and for those with deeper pockets, the threepenny bit tray. The quality and size (something that mattered greatly to us kids) of the sweets increased in line with the value of the tray.

There was another shop on the corner of Longford Road and Lindfield Road, called Bennet's that was much bigger than the one opposite the school gates and stocked a much wider variety of goods. It was Dad's birthday and we were "going out for the day" for a run into the countryside. Well Marple Ridge for some grass tobogganing with big sheets of cardboard.

Mum sent us into Bennet's with half a crown (two shillings and sixpence) to get something nice for Dad's birthday. On retrospect, limited instructions to a 7 year old and a 5 year old. We told Mrs Bennet the amount we had to spend and she got her threepenny bit tray out and in we dived, selecting such delicacies as flying saucers, sherbet dips, as well as smattering of black jacks, stringy jelly and other such small fare.

Returning to the car with our haul, that was spread across two bags, Mum went ballistic. In her mind, we should have bought some chocolate, like a Mars Bar each, or a full block of Cadbury's Dairy Milk. However, she failed to communicate that to two little boys who couldn't understand why she was so angry and who's only experience until that time was the stuff at our eye level. The penny trays. the chocolate bars were all on a display that was above our heads. Literally.

Dad built us a "Trasher" or "Ragger" which was essentially a box seat on a plank with pram wheels and a pram handle on a swivel at the front to steer it. We would push it along at a great speed and race other groups of kids who had similar ones. At some point they would turn over and we all had varieties of Trasher Rash.... and your clothes would look all ragged....

Jackson's brickyard was just off Windmill Lane. In the 1960's the area surrounded by Mill Lane and Harcourt Street was an enormous series of clay pits, with lots of them flooded. It was a great place to fish for newts, sticklebacks and frogs. We would cart bucketloads of frogspawn, had our own outdoor aquariums made out of old Belfast sinks and tin baths. I am quite sure we kept a lot of local cats well fed on fresh fish...

I remember one of the local "big lads" probably a 13 or 14 year-old, rounding us all up one day to go "ratting" in the brickyard pits. We all had to turn up at the corner of Mill Lane and Windmill Road with weapons at a set time. Broom handles with bits of tin cans hammered into a spear shape and nailed on the end, looking like medieval pikes, catapults complete with ball-bearings or marbles, bows and arrows (with proper deadly tips) and a few of the older teenagers had air rifles. In reality, all the youngsters acted as "beaters" to try and flush out the rats for the teenagers to shoot at them but it was a lot of fun and I don't remember anyone getting shot or stabbed so it must have been a success...

I only did 2 years in the Juniors when we moved to Offerton. The only serious memory of that school was our class teacher, Mr Griffiths, hurting me. During the winter of 1964 or 65, both my brother David and me contracted German Measles and one of the side-effects was it damaged our vision. I only noticed as I couldn't see the chalkboard properly in first year of juniors and so just guessed. My school marks went right down. An intervention involving my parents and my teacher, Mrs Watson, deduced I needed an eye test. So I had one arranged.

The diagnosis was myopia and prescription spectacles. I proper hated them and only used them when necessary. They stayed in my pocket, in my desk or in my school bag until I needed them. It was a big thing for me and something I didn't really get over for a long time, long after I left the Royal Navy that's how much I felt it impacted on me. Blind as a bat without them but I was vain and so they stayed out of sight until I needed them.

So there I am in second year at North Reddish Junior School, in Mr Griffiths class. He had written something on the board and was pacing up and down the classroom randomly selecting pupils to answer questions or observations on what he had written. I couldn't see a thing so thought I would quietly reach into my desk (lift the lid) to get my spectacle case and put my bins on to see the board.

I didn't notice Mr Griffiths come up behind me and as I had my fingers in the desk, he did no more than lift up the lid and let it drop on my fingers, the twat. I shouted out in alarm and dragged my sore hands out of the desk whilst he grabbed my ear and dragged me out of the classroom to bollock me whilst the classroom erupted into howls of laughter.

We ended up in a sort of arbitration meeting with the head (Mr Rook), my Mum and Mr Griffiths to explain the events in the cold light of dawn on another day. He eventually apologised and I had to agree to wear my bins all day in classes, every day. Full of embarrassment and no wonder I had a phobia about wearing glasses.

It would become a recurring theme this, learning important lessons with pain….

Chapter Five

Holidays to the 2 tubs pub in Bury

Mum and Dad were having some work done at the house or something. Anyway, David, our dog Lassie and me were packed off to spend time with my Mum's oldest and most favourite sister Doris and her wonderful ex-Royal Navy Telegraphist husband, Geoff Howard.

Doris and Geoff ran the Two Tubs pub in the centre of Bury. Suitably distanced from our house in Reddish to feel proper foreign to David and me. Though the currency seemed to be the same as ours in Reddish but people spoke differently. Ergo, they must be foreign. We spent one whole week there and numerous weekends. It was great fun.

I can remember we used to climb the massive gates blocking off the pub yard from the road and look out spotting car registrations, which if registered in Bury, all ended in the letters EN. We would try and estimate how many EN plates there would be, then clamber up the gates to spot them and count. BEN, TEN, LEN, DEN, etc... A decent bit of competition. Blind guessing, perhaps based on yesterday's winning score, and betting a dare or a penalty on being declared the winner (and loser) before we climbed the gates and commenced the count.

Aunty Doris was already a legend in our house having taken my Mum and her Sister Freda in when her Dad died. Her Mum had died when she was a toddler and her Dad just before the 2nd world war broke out. So, she would have been about five or six years old. Evidently the family divided up what value was left in the house but no-one wanted to take care of two little girls and the discussion had turned to which orphanage they would be placed in.

Doris, then aged eighteen and married to Geoff who was away at sea in the Royal Navy, would hear no more and took Freda and Mum in. She had miscarried at some point and there never were any more pregnancies, so I guess Mum and Freda were a little like surrogate children but Doris never expressed that. She was just looking after her two little sisters.

Aunty Doris had the patience to teach me to play draughts when I was just four years old. She had never spoken to us in baby talk, just had proper conversations and always listened to what we had to say. We adored her immensely.

So, there we are in the pub. First morning, David and me were both up and about early. Not Aunty Doris and Uncle Geoff. Late nights in the pub always meant lie-ins for them, plus weekend was their busiest time. So, the first Saturday morning we crept downstairs to investigate. I have honestly never ever forgot the smell of stale beer and fag ash that met us when we crept into the bar. I smell stale beer now and it will take me right back to that moment when two little boys were peeping out of the door from the stairs to the living area. Funny.

Even more funny was Mrs Jones the cleaner, who appeared next to us with an upright hoover blasting away and a cat curled up on it getting a cheap thrill..... neither of us could understand how the cat remained curled up as Mrs Jones brutally shoved the upright cleaner along the carpets and under the tables.

Mrs Jones did a deal with us that day. A wonderful piece of kidology. She must have been one of the contributors to the book of life. She had us both crawl under the upholstered bench seating fixed to the wall. Drag out the cigarette packets, cellophane, bits of crisps and nuts and whatever other flotsam and jetsam lay down there in the fluffy dark, so she could brush or hoover it up.

So, what was in it for us, I can almost hear you thinking...... hard cash!

Any coins we found, we could have. We just had to scoop out the crap for her to brush and hoover up. Another commercial lesson I guess. Reward for effort. Pennies, ha'pennies and threepenny bits were all gathered and me and David did a 50/50 share with each other on what we found.

It wasn't a bad deal in the history of child exploitation but it was certainly lucrative in the eyes of our David and me. We got money to spend on stuff we wanted and the thing we craved most at that time was Limeade.

We had never had the luxury of flavoured drinks at home in Reddish but in the Two Tubs in Bury, there were riches beyond a small child's wildest dream. Drinks of all sorts of colours. Not like the alcopop revolution of recent decades but still, very colourful in its day.

We did all sorts of odd jobs and favours to get the reward of a glass of limeade, with a piece of ice in to have it really cold. No fridge in Reddish, unless you count the whole house, where we could make ice-lollies in the pantry.

So, one Saturday we have spent our first hour or so providing "free" help and support to Mrs Jones. Had our glass of limeade when Uncle Geoff opened the bar and went outside to play. The pub had a big old barn that was full of old furniture, a car under a canvas cover, step ladders and remnants of many parties and events, piled up on top of each other and all covered in dust. We weren't supposed to be in there but with Doris and Geoff tending the bar on a busy day, we had room to manoeuvre.

David was rummaging around in a bit of furniture at the back of the barn and as he felt the drawer lining in one, he noticed it was a bit lumpy. He peeled back the old wallpaper or whatever had been used to create the drawer lining and underneath was a handful of "tanners" (6d pieces) or what we thought were tanners. We ran back into the pub to show Aunty Doris or Uncle Geoff what we had found and spend our treasure on Limeade but encountered a savvy regular on his way to the lavvy.

Hey up lads what have you got there he asked. David showed him the coins and he said what we were going to do with them. We excitedly said we wanted a glass of limeade each. He shook his head and said it wasn't quite enough for two and offered to buy them for us by adding some of his own money. Wait out in the yard and he would bring them out. Which he did.

So, there we are, sat in the sun feeling really good for ourselves sipping our ice-cold limeade when Aunty Doris came out and asked where we had got the drinks from. We told the story and a little sceptical, we led her to the cabinet in the barn and the drawer where we had found the coins. Doris rummaged round and found 3 more, Victorian silver threepenny bits. Not tanners. Then worth five or six times a silver sixpence… so whilst we had been short changed, I don't quite see it as robbery, though we did learn another commercial lesson…. Understand the value of what you have before you give it away….

I lost contact with David Gibson when I was 10 and about a year after we moved house. I tried many times to try and find him, using social media, the primary school old pupils Facebook page etc. so that we could fill each other in with our life stories but without success. It was whilst writing the first chapters of this book during the Covid-19 assault on the

UK in the spring of 2020 that I discovered he had passed away from cancer of the oesophagus only the week before "I found him". I cried.

Chapter Six

Offerton Neighbourhood Estate

Mum and Dad had been on the council housing list to move property for a long time. Mum was successful after mithering the housing office and we finally moved from "the fridge" in Reddish to the modern day living of a centrally heated brand-new house at Malham Court on Offerton Estate in 1966.

I remember padding round in my bare feet in wonder of the warmth that first winter. The central heating was via warm air venting, coming off a central boiler based in the kitchen. It was World Cup year and also the same time that Dad finished being a lorry driver and started work as a bus driver with North Western, on more money. Things were looking up.

The estate was a new-build local authority housing project, finally numbering over a thousand homes. In the 1960's house building boom, the main estate was constructed during the 1960's and early 1970's and built on what is known as the "Radburn Principles" which focus on a great number of cul-de-sacs with walk ways and green spaces.

Everyone's house number was based on the road the house backed onto, with the fronts facing out onto open-planned landscapes of lawns and shrubberies.

Offerton Hall Primary School was an early completion, although the playing fields remained a muddy bog for a year whilst the grass-seed took and eventually spawned a junior football pitch.

The estate wasn't that green either in the mid-60's as hundreds of houses were under construction at the same time. Not like today, with fenced and boarded off building sites, it was a mishmash of building construction, with materials stored on any land left for the future green space. A massive pile of concrete drainage pipes at the side of the house opposite was a great place for a youngster to play "war" and defend the pill boxes.

There was scaffolding up at the town houses being constructed just a few hundred yards from our house on Crosswaite Road, creating the most amazing climbing frames, we would swing from them, climb them and jump off onto the big piles of sand at each end of the terraces. The whole building area had one old British Legion security guard in a hut that "protected" the most expensive construction materials but the rest was fair game.

We used to play "war" a lot. Sometimes cowboys and Indians, sometimes it was the second world war. You would "shoot" someone and say bang or something like that and wonder why the other boy you had "shot" dead centre in the chest or head, protested that it had only skimmed his arm and therefore he was only wounded and could carry on fighting himself.

To solve all the arguments, we bought rubber dart guns. Push the dart into the gun, fire it (at close range) and you could see the dart hit the victim. Body or head shot was an undeniable kill. Arms or legs hit you had to assume a wound and they could carry on fighting.

This lasted all about one summer until everyone's darts got lost or broke in the hand to hand fighting that would invariably develop. We then moved onto the next stage of evolution "clay bullets" and a stick.

The gas central heating venting chambers used to get really hot and were great for cooking clay bullets on. We would gather the clay (in abundance around the estate) roll it into a long thin sausage, cut with scissors, roll into bullet shapes that fit your own particular dart gun and leave overnight to dry on the vents. Proper ammo.

When you hit someone, there was even a burst of blood (dust as the clay bullet disintegrated) on your victim and you could see exactly who got shot, where they got shot and whether they were wounded or not. Either way, bullets spent, we would always resort to hand to hand fighting anyway.

Someone got a clay bullet in the eye. No lasting damage but some of the parents colluded, we all got bollocked and the "sekedin" guns, spud guns, dart guns, bows and arrows etc. all got confiscated. We therefore needed a new way of ensuring a hit. Weeds.

The big tall purple weeds (official name is Rosebay willow herb or Fireweed) would grow to a height of about five feet. We used to pull them out carefully so the whole root came (prized element). Strip off all the leaves and break down into 3 or 4 throwing sticks. "Sticks and stones may break my bones" but they sure as hell were the thing for playing war. They hurt when you got hit by one.

We saved the root balls for last as they made pretty good clubs for hand to hand fighting. You would see kids walking round with 4 or 5 root ball sticks stuck in their pants or belts. Some would be thrown, and they proper hurt but a final one was always kept for the last elements of the fight.

Storming the pill box or the castle (derelict and haunted pub on Marple Road), which was located on the edge of the construction site, near to the posh private houses. Hand to hand fighting would deteriorate into wrestling or a proper fight with punches thrown. No pansies on our estate.

The house my Mum had managed to secure for our new family home was the end one of a terrace. It had 3 manhole covers in what Mum wanted as a lawn. Must have been where all the street drains converged. All very unsightly.

Workmen laying flagstones at different parts of the estate had a few accidents and Mum noticed the broken ones not being used. When she asked if she could have the bits for a crazy paving path in her garden, she got the nod. Probably because it was less rubbish to dispose of and their logistics and works order process must have allowed for breakages.

She made a start on the path but ran of bits. My brother David and I were sent out to scour other parts of the estate that were being built to find other broken bits for the path. We proper struggled and could only find whole ones. However, push one or two over and they break into "broken bits".

We loaded up our Trasher (plank of wood with pram wheels and a T-shaped front set steered by a pram handle) and went home. Mum was pleased. So, we broke another half a dozen or more and carried the pieces back. As I said, security was at a minimum. All the brickies and labourers knocked off work at 4pm and went home, just as we were coming out of school. The timing couldn't have been better!

Playing war in the drainage pipe dump one day, I fell off the top of the pile and my leg caught the edge of a pipe on the way down. Cutting through my welly boot, my jeans and making a right mess of my shin. Chipped the shin bone and it took 4 stitches to seal the wound. God knows what would have happened if I didn't have my trusty wellies on. Wellies were standard fare on the estate at that time. No proper paths, mud everywhere and on everything. It was after all a building site but also our playground.

We were playing one of our war games, which involved the taking of a fort. The fort in this question was a massive pile of timber being used to create the roofs of the houses on Otterburn Place. Some of the kids were on top and throwing sticks down and others throwing stuff up and firing bows and arrows when the security guard came out of his hut. Quite an old guy and we all knew we could easily outrun him normally but on this occasion, he sort of arrived immediately and shouted. We all scattered.

My brother David was looking back at the guard as he ran away and wasn't looking where he was going. At full pelt he ran into a pile of timber beams. One of them speared his knee and he stopped dead, impaled on the wood and started screaming. We all stopped running and went back to help him. The security guard nearly fainted and wobbled off back to his hut to call an ambulance.

A piece of the wood was embedded in David's knee and it took the guard and an ambulanceman to carefully get him off the wood, into the ambulance and off to hospital. His knee was a mess and was a constant weakness for him as long as he lived. One of several areas of his body that was attacked mercilessly when he was very ill before he passed away a long time later but when he was still young...

When Dad wasn't working he loved to read. He enrolled us into Great Moor library within weeks of arriving on the estate. Our nearest one and it was over a mile away from our house. I went once and didn't like it. David was an avid book reader from a very early age. I remember Mum instructing Dad to get us both down the library for some books. I wasn't having it.

Dad had massive hands and did this thing where he formed his thumb and forefinger into a circle around our wrists, like a handcuff and would just drag us, kicking and screaming until he slapped us but his grip was immense and no pulling or squirming could you get out of it.

So, he drags us down Lisburne Lane and Cherry Tree Lane to the library on Gladstone Street. Although it was only me being dragged. David trotted along quite willingly. He may even have skipped some of the way.

I got dumped onto a seat inside the entrance with instructions not to move as he and David went off to select the books they were going to read over the two or three week loan period. I just sat there with my arms folded and bottom lip stuck out. Boring books.

The librarian on duty kept looking over at me as she stamped in and recorded the returned books from a big pile on her desk. When she finished she came over and sat beside me. She asked me what was the matter and I explained that I found books boring and just wanted to play outside. She seemed to agree with me that playing out was good. She then asked me what I did on rainy days.

I told her about listening to music on Dads radiogram (monster unit with a big speaker in it) and watching action films on the telly. Oh, she asked, what sort of action films. So, I told her about two Viking films that had made a big impression on me. “The Vikings” and “The Long Ships” full of adventure and fighting, like what I did when I played with my mates.

Okay she said, come with me and walked us over to a section of the library and introduced me to Leif Erikson and the Viking sagas. She said try one of these, they are all about the Vikings. So, I started with him and Dad signed the book out to me.

I devoured it. I loved the action, the exploration and the stories. I couldn’t wait to get back to the library and the next volumes and so moved onto his Dad Erik the Red, then the Viking sagas and by the time I was about twelve or thirteen, I was a regular visitor at the library with David and we always had two or three books on the go at home. I have never stopped reading ever since then and owe a great deal to a librarian who had the patience to connect with me that day.

I formed and managed a football team made up of all the kids who lived near to and faced onto Crosswaite Road and called ourselves Crosswaite Athletic. Mixed age group but mainly eleven to thirteen year olds. We played other teams from across the estate. None of us had any proper kits and we would negotiate on what colour we would wear. Then an instruction went out to rest of the team to turn up at “Wembley” in a red shirt, or a blue shirt. No-one had any other colours and nobody would be mad enough to wear white. Most games were good natured affairs, some degenerated into mass brawls.

“Wembley” was the only grass pitch on the estate in the first year or so, then the grass finally seeded on the school pitch to double our opportunities of a game.

Chapter Seven

RS McColl Newsagents

My first job was delivering papers from a newsagent's a mile or so from our house on Hempshaw Lane. I loved it. The pay was bobbins though and a controversial "Xmas Tips" scheme when I got only a fraction of what I tipped into the communal bucket was a joke and I left. Honesty doesn't always pay was another lesson I learned.

As the Offerton Neighbourhood Estate was being constructed, a small shopping precinct was also built, comprising a supermarket, butchers, chemist, newsagent, greengrocers, a couple of fashion shops, a haberdashery and a hardware store.

I remember the excitement when Freddy Garrity, of Freddie and the Dreamers (1960's pop band) opened a children's fashion shop in the precinct. Lots of local press on the day. I don't now if he owned it or not but I think the shop was titled off one of his records, Little Red Donkey. Way too ahead for a council estate and it didn't last that long really, maybe four or five years.

People off the estate generally shopped for clothes on Stockport Market in those days. Fashion shops were well posh for us council house folks.... Ha ha.

I applied for a job at the newsagents, a family enterprise called "Mellors" but later bought out by the then rapidly expanding RS McColl, just McColl these days. The owner sold up but remained as manager of the outlet or maybe it was an early franchise arrangement. Mrs Mellor, a lovely lady.

I used to get to the shop as early as she did and help set up each of the paper rounds by selecting the newspapers and marking them up to a list and bagging them up ready for the rest of the paperboys (no girls employed in those days). Mrs Mellor would have me doing that rather than let me out early on my round as she always feared the council's inspector from bubbling her for a big fine.

Riding my bike was a big part of my life and had been since I was about 7 or 8 years old. I would ride everywhere. Delivering newspapers just seemed a normal extension of what I did. I would grab my paper bag and set off in wild abandon, regardless of the weather. Remember, it's not a question of the wrong weather for an activity but the wrong choice of clothing.

If it was sunny, I didn't have a coat on. If it rained, I had a coat on. If it snowed I put a hat and gloves on, as well as a coat. Not woollen gloves because it was a bind trying to get the newspapers out. I used to borrow my Mum's leather gloves. Tight fitting, they would grip a newspaper and I could shove them through a letterbox really easily. Mum got printers ink from the gloves fingers on her coat one day, which resulted in her "presenting" them to me and buying herself some new ones.... Bonus.

As I set off, I would select my newspaper read for the run. Sometimes the Daily Mirror, sometimes the Daily Mail. As I got to that newspaper, I would cycle no-handed and scan the headlines. Sometimes stopping to read the article before I posted the paper. I do remember reading an account of a baby that had climbed out of its cot, out through an open window and a paper boy had saved its life when it clung onto a window frame. I thought that I could one day be such a hero.

So, one summer's morning as I was on the outer reaches of my round, I heard a proper commotion. A woman screaming up one of the cul-de-sacs off my route. I turned my bike into the road and saw a woman being dragged out of a garden and into a car. A man at the gate was trying to pull her back inside and a guy trying to force her into the car. Shit. What should I do?

I thought I had to show willing, even a 13-year old versus adults and shouted up the road to see if any help was needed. All three of them, almost in unison, told me to Fuck Off. So, I did.... I think it was the first real "domestic" I had ever seen.

A year later, our David reached the age where he too could be a paper boy and we would both race to get up, out and down to the shop. We shared the same bedroom. The precinct was only a few hundred yards from our house, down a hill. So, it was a competition to be first, or not be last. Same thing really. Isn't everything in the life of sibling rivalry?

We would race down, hang a left into the fully paved area and peg it to the newsagents, then brake hard and skid the bike down on one side, come to a stop let the momentum bring you and the bike upright and rollover, we would step off as it rolled over and lowered it the last foot or so by one handlebar, so it was left on the floor, on its side and step off all in one fluid smooth movement. A pretty cool move that we had both perfected.

However, this one particular morning our David had got a good lead on me and was going to win, he looked over his shoulder to me with a victory grin but left his braking a tad late. So, when he braked and laid the bike down, instead of sliding to a halt he hit the plate glass window at full tilt, which shattered.

Thankfully David did not sustain any serious injury, only some minor cuts and bruises and a big heap of embarrassment. I calmly slid the bike into the correct position and strolled through the door with a victory nod to myself and a look at the startled and speechless Mrs Mellor.

Insurance covered the replacement window but David had to pay the excess. A tenner. A lot of money then and my Dad skimmed his paperboy wages for many weeks to pay off the tenner he gave to Mrs Mellor. We both got major bollockings from our Dad and Mrs Mellor about how we skidded to a halt. Not sure we actually stopped but reached a truce on racing to the shop, which probably masked that we kept on doing it anyway. It did look cool. Skidding to a stop, laying the bike on its side and stepping off, all in one smooth move. Not many others could manage it.

It didn't stop us both racing and competing on other things. In the pre-technology days, David and I had a number of different games we competed against each other with. The dictionary game was one of them, quite a placid game.

One of us flicks the big desk dictionary and the other says stop. Columns one to four, choose one. Words in that column are eight or whatever, choose a number. The person with the dictionary would then say the word and the other had to spell it and explain what it meant. It was a good game and turned us both into wordsmiths. He more than I, as he went on to University and became an English teacher.

Our weekend game was to get from our beds to the living room downstairs, without touching the carpet. The finishing line was the carpet tread separating the living room from the hall. Climbing over chests of drawers was the easy bit. Hanging like a limpet with bare feet on the skirting board holding onto anything we could as we inched towards the stairs, was the challenging bit.

We each had our own route round the bedroom and to the stairs but it was a foregone conclusion that the first person onto the bannister would win. Usually accompanied by a triumphant low cheer by the leader. Low because we clearly did not want to alert the parents as we damaged wallpaper and Dad couldn't understand why his painted skirting board had scuffs and cracks on it....

David reached the stairs ahead of me on one such morning and was inching down the bannisters getting to the newel at the bottom, where he would make the turn, inch on and then step into the living room. However, instead of dutifully accepting defeat and inching down in convoy I saw that the living room door was already open and thought I could jump from the other side of the bannister directly into the living room.

Physics and geometry however, intercepted initiative. I saw the look of despair on David's face as I climbed over the bannister and launched myself towards and over the carpet tread in the doorway but that clearly changed as my forehead hit the wall over the door frame and I dropped backwards onto the hall carpet like a sack of potatoes. His victory smile as he used my breathless prone body as a stepping-stone into the living room was priceless.

One summers day we cycled from Offerton to Marple locks. A series of tough hills to navigate which led to us both "dying of thirst" before we got up the last major hurdle "Dan Bank" and continued with the gentler incline up into the village. We had some spends, not much. A penny and a ha'penny each. I suggested that if we pooled our money, we could buy a threepenny iced lolly. David replied yes but what will you have..... I nearly fell off my bike. I had meant to share between us. Little bugger.

David and I had begun to argue and fight. A phase that lasted long after we both left home. He to University and me to join the Royal Navy but before then, we had good times and we had bad times. Dad used to give us both a good slapping and neither he nor our Mum could understand and effectively manage, our sibling rivalry. I don't think we understood it either. We just did some things out of spite sometimes....

In 1969, we had a wonderful surprise. Our little brother Ged was born. He was and still is adored and loved by everyone but at that time, he also provided a distraction to the sibling rivalry thing. David spent a lot of time reading books with Ged, sharing his knowledge and understanding of literature in a way I couldn't.

I used to take Ged playing football and spent ages with him teaching him how to control a ball and pass a ball with both feet. Wrestling and playing with soldiers and tanks. He got tons of love from both of us.

Not known for taking a risk in the culinary department, however Mum's Sunday roast was to die for and none of us were allowed to leave the table until our plates were clean. Ever. A leftover from our parent's experiences with food rationing during and after the Second World War, meant we couldn't waste a thing.

Mid-week would be standard fare of sausage and mash, boiled pork ribs with bread and butter, beans on toast and a particular speciality of Malham Court, Beans in a Dish. It did exactly what it said on the side of the tin, to coin a phrase. A bowlful of Heinz 57 and a side plate of two buttered rounds of white bread. You don't get that fine a fare everywhere for sure.

We never had any alcohol in the house. It was only at Christmas were any of us allowed a "drink" and there was a choice of a glass of sherry or half a pint of stout. I always chose the stout as there was more in it, I liked the bitter taste and was never a real fan of sweet tasting drinks, though David was.

My newspaper round didn't provide sufficient funds for my new-found hobby as a 14-year old. Going into pubs. It was actually a little before I was 14 because I did celebrate my 14th birthday with five pints of bitter in the George Hotel in Stockport town centre. The only pub we could get served in at the time. The landlady let us sit in a corner of one of the bars as long we didn't draw attention to ourselves. It was 10p a pint and my entire wages of 50p was gone in a flash. I knew then I would need to earn more money.

Chapter Eight

Champion Bakery

Just before Christmas 1971, I got a Saturday job delivering bread with my Stockport County mad cousin Bobby Jeffries who worked at Champion Bakery, Longshut Lane, Stockport and worked with him for about 2 months. Bobby wore thick black national health framed glasses and always sported a blue and white scarf from his beloved County. A very pragmatic lad.

Bobby's round was the gigantic Manchester overspill estate built at the wonderful location of Hattersley, on the cusp of the Peak District. It was a shithole. I did the paper round for a few more weeks but gave it up as the money on the bread round was better and for only one-day a week.

In the run up to Christmas the Depot Manager got all the drivers in the big shed and stood on a bit of a balcony to give them their pre-delivery briefing. A lot of waffle from my perspective but his two key messages were to sell as much additional stuff as possible. Not just bread, we could offer milk, potatoes and some other standard items. So, it was a sell, sell, sell thing. His second message also seemed very sensible, no more slates. Meaning, no more credit to those who owed lots of money. Get the cash in, that was important.

We got into the van and Bobby gave me his interpretation. Sell as much stuff as possible, get orders in, no matter what they owe, get the orders in. Debt collection is someone else's problem, not ours.

So off we trotted to the shit hole of Hattersley and got stuck in. I asked everyone if they needed any potatoes or milk and stuff and Bobby was pleased with the additional orders we took. He was happy because he was on sales commission whilst I was on a fixed wage of about £2. Good money in my eyes but hey ho.

I knocked on one door and it slowly opened as the entire lock had been smashed in, as the door was presumably kicked in from last night's domestic entertainment. I looked at Bobby's debt list and it was bigger than my wage! Given that a loaf of bread was about 10p god only knows what else they had added to their "slate". Anyway I shouted that I needed to collect some of the debt and a deep male voice shouted down the stairs "Fuck off" and as I started to walk away it continued "Leave the loaf you wanker and add 5lb of spuds next week"...... what a place.

In early 1972 I got a second job and had to give up the bread round as the all-day Saturday thing was a clash. The new job was at Lipton's Supermarket in the corner of the precinct. Thursday, Friday evening after school and all-day Saturday. Proper income of £4.50 a week to pay for the increasing desire to socialise.

Chapter Nine

Lipton's Supermarket & Stockport Technical High School for Boys

From 1972 until 1974 I worked in the butcher's department of Lipton's Supermarket, in the precinct on Offerton Neighbourhood Estate. The whole precinct was demolished and eventually replaced by an Aldi.

I worked there part-time in my last years at school and full-time in the period from May to December 1974 when I joined the Royal Navy. The estate was a tough old place, with many families re-housed there from a number of designated slum areas around Stockport that were demolished in the 1960's and 1970's.

There were lots of different gang factions around even then, that in the modern day have since flourished into protection rackets and the management of complex drug selling rings... More naive in the 1970's it was mainly violence, vandalism and breaking and entering in those early days.

I had my own run-ins as I was never part of the in-crowd, having passed my 11+ exam and attended Stockport Technical High School for boys. Whilst everyone else seemed to go to Dialstone Lane Secondary School.

So, in 1969 I passed my 11+ examination. Eleven-plus had been introduced in 1944 as a national test to examine a student's ability to solve problems using verbal and non-verbal reasoning. It was associated with the "Tripartite System" until largely phased out by 1976. The exam was used to determine which type of school the student should attend after primary education, a grammar school, a secondary school or a technical school. I had the full choice but selected Stockport Technical High School for Boys. Set in a campus with Offerton Girls (Secondary School) and Goyt Bank High School for Girls.

I performed very well in the first two years at school. Finishing head of year in 1970 and second in 1971 but I didn't like the attention I received from my peers. I didn't want to identify with being a brainbox after seeing my little brother David castigated at primary school by bullies, where he earned the nickname "The Professor" because he knew so much.

Therefore, I made a conscious decision to step out of the limelight of being bright and turn my energy into humour, whilst continuing to stand up for myself. Not slow in expressing my opinions I said what I saw and acted accordingly. This resulted in learning some good things and a lot of not so good things.....

Dinnertime at the High School was a fraught affair. Mr Whitehouse the Head had instigated some form of mentoring I think, with tables set out separately for 5th and 6th formers but the rest were ordered into 2 first form at the end, 2 second form, then 2 third form and finally heading the table of 8 were two 4th formers who were responsible for dividing up the slosh provided by the dinner ladies.

Portion servings were therefore, Biafra for first formers, China for second formers, England for third formers and USA for the 4th form servers. The twats on our table had a routine of dividing up the pies or stew accordingly but making sure the gravy washed all around the plate so that a patrolling teacher glancing over would think that everyone had a full plate. That went on for a long time and I remember complaining and reaching out for a sausage on the rare day we had them and got a fork jabbed into the back of my hand for the trouble.

I stood up and slapped the offender, who was a good foot taller and 3 years older than me. It alerted the attention of the teachers and both of us were escorted out. I cannot remember the lads name but I made a point of giving him a sly punch (from the side or behind) whenever I could and got a good battering by him and his mates in return. It lasted a whole year until he left school at 15 and got a job somewhere. Wanker. I was a fast runner though and avoided most of their attempts on me.

I did get whacked on the back of the head with a lacrosse stick one lunchtime. The blow struck me at the base of my neck and top of my spine. It didn't just knock me out, I was temporarily paralysed and spent the rest of the day in Accident & Emergency at Stockport Infirmary. The lad who did it got a bollocking and a temporary suspension from school. Like lots of things, it didn't last long.

My running got me into the schools cross-country team in the winter and I ran 100m, 200m and 400m athletics in the summer. Representing the school, I got into a number of finals without ever winning anything of note.

I also wanted to play football and the PE Teacher, Albert Renshaw, who had an affliction of sucking air in through clenched teeth that made a sort "csssheeeeesch" sound, let me join training and the year squad in third form but didn't like that it clashed with cross-country, where he seemed to have high hopes for me. I wasn't its greatest fan. Always having had poor circulation in my hands, I used to get that cold (and muddy) that I wasn't able to untie the laces of my running shoes to get changed before going home.

Albert clearly had a strategy that I failed to recognise then, though perhaps now understand. He made me substitute in the football team. In a time when there was only one sub, it was me. He made me stand and watch the game for 90 minutes without ever putting me on the pitch. He did the same the following week and for the next 7 games. At no point did he ever speak to me about it. Just had me as a non-playing sub. I refused to go back to cross-country running but did continue with my athletics in the summer.

Those of us not getting in the team, Bob Allison and me in particular, decided to create our own football team. We made some enquiries but found out we needed adults to represent us. Ian Collins said his Dad would do it. So, for one season we formed a team and played under the Collins local diocese in Heaton Moor and called ourselves St. Pauls.

The team started off well and we were all playing regularly. Then the manager started bringing in sons of his friends. One of them was a young Nigel Hart, a year younger than us and went on to play professionally. His Dad Johnny Hart was at City and used to turn up with kit and boots for us all to buy at knockdown prices.

The manager had some odd selection habits which usually revolved around the availability of his superstars. I played wing half when I did get on. He asked me to play right wing in one game and I scored five goals. He dropped me the following week as his star winger was then back from holiday. When I asked why can't I get a run out at wing half then and he said that couldn't drop the lad who played there as he had done so well…… I do remember thinking what the fuck?

By the end of the season, the lads who formed the team weren't getting a game anymore, so we wrapped our hands in and didn't see the season out.

At some point in the academic calendar, not sure when, the school presented its "colours" to all its sporting hero's. The football team all got them, the cross-country running squad all got them and the athletes got them. All except for me….. cheers Albert. It was the first of a series of steps where I believed the school were slowly trying to piss me off and it worked.

Albert was good for one thing in my mind, he was a fairly decent tennis coach and everything I know about the game I learned from him. How to hold the racquet properly for maximum control, how to play back hand and fore hand and the arc you need your arms to flow in to pinpoint where you want the ball to go.

A group of us played tennis all summer in the lunch times at school. Taking over the courts and running a "ladder" (a divisional table) where you progressed up or down the ladder depending on the result of your one lunchtime game. It was great fun and it cascaded over into my out of school activities for a couple of years at least. My brother David, my mates the Platts (Paul & Mark) some of the Henshall's and co would cycle back to school and play in the tennis courts of Offerton Girls school. They had more courts than the other 2 schools on the campus but it was right next the caretakers house.

The caretaker was a canny ex-soldier and let us play tennis, as long as we didn't climb the fences to retrieve lost balls and that no other kids could play by the school buildings at anything. So, during those evenings we became his de facto security guards. Maintaining a watch out on the buildings whilst playing endless sets of tennis. A fair deal and yet another example of you scratch my back and I will scratch yours which would become a feature of my commercial negotiations later in life. WIIFM (What's In It For Me) a wonderful life lesson.

In a small world many, many years later, the caretaker's granddaughter married my youngest son.

Winters would be a bind and quite often we would have to find "indoor" play to keep us occupied. We had chess drives and played every board game under the sun but they were not particularly satisfying from my perspective. I liked my toy soldiers but it wasn't a thing for boys of a certain age so I devised a form of table top war gaming based on the content of a book I won for being top of the year in my first year at Stockport Tech. I still have the book.

I made up the first set of rules, which included a schedule of how far a group of soldiers could march, a tank could advance under fire. The rate of fire, the damage, etc. all had scores. We used spent ice lolly sticks as measures and had a fistful of dice. We took it in turns to throw the dice in an attacking phase with the other throwing defence scores to limit the casualties. It was hugely successful and Mum's across our group were more than happy to host our games. We used plasticine to lay out "barbed wire" obstacles or defensive positions, pill boxes etc. The rules were modified after reaching impasse in a few situations and became our winter game of choice.

In the autumn of my second year at Stockport Tech, my estate mates The Platts and our David used to go exploring the woods around the schools and further afield. We had heard a rumour about "Conker Wood" a magical place that you could sit in one place and fill a large carrier bag with enormous brightly coloured conkers. Ha ha. It really did exist and we found it. It was spread across two sides of a little valley.

On one of our regular jaunts there, a walk down Marple Road and ask a farmer for permission to cross his land, which we did. We were in there. Someone else had fitted a rope swing off one of the chestnut tree boughs and it was great for swinging out across the valley. We then dropped off into piles of leaves and mush.

I must have got my hands a bit too muddy and that combined with a challenge to walk as far back up the hill as possible to get a monster swing caused a physics phenomenon where the weight of swung object creates a greater force than the muddy hands can control and I slid off the rope swing at its zenith….

There was a movie of the day called "Those Magnificent Men in their Flying Machines" and it had a catchy song about flying through the air with the greatest of ease and flying upside down with their feet in the air and don't really care. Well they would if they landed like I did. Back first. About 30 feet down from the end of the rope.

It knocked all the wind out of me and I was struggling to breathe. The first person to react properly was my brother David and he whacked me in the back with all his might, that caused me to gasp and inhale again. Then flop back down into the mud and leaves. I was in absolute agony and the pains in my back were awful.

The Platts ran back up the valley, across the field to the farmer and he in turn called for an ambulance. It took a while for them all to work out how to get me up and out of conker wood, across the field and into the ambulance in the farmyard. I was strapped into a wheelchair and they used a winch on the front of the tractor to slowly haul me out. Then put me onto a stretcher on his tractor to get across the fields and then into the ambulance and off to hospital.

After being X-Rayed and examined it was determined that I had split my spleen. A pretty serious thing evidently. So, I went on a no-food diet and drinks were limited to water only for the first 3 days before the medical people revised the diagnosis to a bruised spleen. Never mind about the bruised back. I was black and blue from my neck to and including my buttocks.

For whatever reason, the children's wards were all full and I as a twelve / thirteen year-old was placed into a wing of a men's ward. I had a whale of a time. There was a lovely old guy in the next bed who was recovering from a hernia operation. It took him absolutely ages to walk to the toilet and I thought it was hilarious that his name was Mr Fleet, as he was anything but….

Another couple of guys told me I would come in handy once I could get up and out of my bed. Oh yeh, I thought, what is this all about. They asked me if I liked apples. I said yes, who doesn't. Great they said, come with us.

We walked out of the ward, all in pyjamas, dressing gowns and slippers, down the corridor to a little quadrangle thing. A small orchard surrounded by buildings on all four sides. One of the guys helped me clamber up onto the shoulders of the tallest and start ripping apples off. Ha ha. It seemed they had been at it for days but all the low hanging fruit had been picked. A little bit of ingenuity and a lightly weighted teenager enabled the ward to have fresh fruit most days. Top stuff.

The food was definitely not worth shouting about. On the fourth day when they let me eat after the period of observation was over (and I was Hank Marvin), I was handed a menu. I could choose from a selection. I had never been in a café or a restaurant or anywhere like it and was staggered that I could choose something. I thought I would pick the best. Rabbit caught my eye and so that's what I ordered. Welsh rabbit. Perhaps it tasted better than English rabbit, who knows?

When my cheese on toast arrived and I complained about not having any rabbit. Mr Fleet nearly popped his stitches as he howled with laughter…. Welsh Rarebit it stated…. Not rabbit. Another lesson in life. Read the words carefully Perkins and don't be afraid of asking questions….. All told, I was off school about 6 weeks. Convalescing at home, mainly until the bruising went and the internal pains ebbed away.

When I was back up and about, the principles of our family to pay respects and say our thank you's compelled me to go and see the farmer (and probably nudged by Mum). I thanked him very much for his help and for the few years that we continued to use Conker Wood we had that affinity and would always exchange greetings with him and his family. Lovely people.

I didn't realise how hard the time off school would hit me until we got to the spring and we had to choose the subjects we would take to GCE O-Level and the qualifications we would need to be successful as an adult. Or so the theory goes.

All my experience of playing war with school friends, my table top gaming and watching war movies plus the key role models in my life (Dad and Uncles who had been in the War or completed their National Service) had all shared their military experiences with me, they were funny, sad, good and bad and had made a big impression on me. It certainly whetted my appetite and my intent to join the forces was slowly cultivated. I knew what I wanted to do and nothing was going to get in my way.

I wanted to go into a technical role in the military. I of course did my homework and knew that I needed to have at least two technical GCE O-Levels. At Stockport Tech, each year had a maximum of 60 boys. The technical subjects were limited to 30 for Technical Drawing (a must for me) with 15 of those 30 doing metal work and the other 15 doing woodwork. There was something else for other 30 but as it didn't apply to me I ignored it...

So, there we are as a year, all 60 boys sat in the assembly hall with the Headmaster, Mr Whitehouse (or Dobber to us kids due his enormous bald head) and most of his teachers, to unravel the problem. The problem was that all 60 boys had chosen Technical Drawing. Chosen for a number of reasons. The teacher was a cracking guy Mr Plant and a lot of the lads wanted to get into the big engineering companies like Simons and Mirlees, who employed thousands in Stockport. Though they don't anymore.

It was decided that the 30 places would be determined by metalwork first. Then the most senior of skills in the Tech. Mr Beeston the metal work teacher stated that all the boys had done well but it was only fair to award the 15 places on the most consistent of attendee's and skills demonstrated over the last year. By virtue of my missing 6 weeks. I had failed to get to grips with the first two assignments as I had not practiced them properly. I was probably bottom of the list of 60 and therefore didn't feature in the 15 named by Mr Beeston.

The remaining 45 boys then all chose woodwork. This was now my best chance and it lay in the choice of Mr Lister, the woodwork teacher. Another lovely guy. He said that he wouldn't use assignments and attendance, as everyone had tried so hard and woodwork could be such an unforgiving subject when all your hard work could be undone by a misplaced chisel or overly enthusiastic blow with a hammer. He would select names from a hat.

Raffles have never been a positive selection tool in my experience and none more so than that day as he chose 15 names from a hat. None of them included me. I looked around in alarm as to what that meant for me. I was a bit numb when the Headmaster announced that the other 30 would now be enrolled in Economics and Bookkeeping..... I had a proper "What the Fuck" moment, as I realised that this would be a serious blow to my military ambitions.

I went to see my form tutor, who arranged for a meeting with my Mum, Dad and Dobber the Headmaster. He listened patiently to my plea that I needed to attain a suitable technical qualification if I was to realise my ambition's. Dobber then announced something that I was a little aware of but hadn't understood the implications. The following year we were going to merge with the two girl's schools alongside us and form Goyt Bank a new comprehensive secondary school and the number of places in all technical subjects would be increased. I just had to wait a year.

Bookkeeping and Economics were largely wasted on me and I really just saw it as "marking time" until I could get back into the technical subjects. I understood double entry bookkeeping after about a month. After that it was just so repetitive that it did challenge my resolve but I stuck at it. It did come in handy when I took up the role of Treasurer in an amateur football club but that was a long way away from then. I had no desires to work in accountancy.

I patiently did my time and when it came to the end of third year, we could choose again. Guess what, more controversy. I could have Technical Drawing but all the spare metal and wood work places would be going to girls to give them a taste of boy stuff. Home economics and baking lessons were on offer to encourage boys in other subjects, but of no use to me at that time. I hastily revised my choices to do Technical Drawing and Art. At least it would give me the qualifications to pick up a role of cartographer in the RAF but not the flight engineer role I thought I wanted.

No, you cannot do Art came the response from the educational hierarchy, as it clashes with your German. That's okay I said, I will drop German but my form tutor Mr Butcher was also the German teacher and said he wouldn't let it happen, I was one of his best students. Fuck me. I needed to bring the big guns back in. So, there we are in yet another big pow wow in Dobbers office. The Headmaster, my Dad, my form tutor, my year Head, Mr Harris and the Art Teacher, Mr Hall.

It all came down to a choice between Art and German. I wanted to do Art. I needed to do Art, otherwise Technical Drawing was wasted. The decision it appeared rested with Mr Hall who uttered the most damning and deceitful statement I think I ever heard from a schoolteacher. Sorry Mr Perkins, your son has no imagination. Best he sticks with German. Didn't matter a jot what I thought. That was it. Everyone rubberstamped Nobby's assessment and my Dad took me home. No imagination, I drew a fucking cartoon for the Royal Family in 1977 but that was yet to come.

I felt proper fucked over. So, what did I do? I resorted to being a scallywag of course. Disruptive in classes, all classes. Can I go for a smoke Miss. No you cannot. Please Miss. No and if you mention it again I will send you to see the headmaster. Great, I can have a smoke on the way..... setting fire to things in chemistry. Nicking off school and vandalising stuff in my spare time.

The only two teachers who I had any respect for were Mrs Bannister who not only took us for English and did so very well but was ever so fit and a bit of a sex symbol to a lot of us. The other one was our year one tutor Fred Alexander a pragmatic and very direct speaking fella from the north east who played rugby. I lost respect for everyone else because they showed zero interest in my career ambitions. It felt a lot like they were just ticking boxes.

The period of self-imposed resistance coincided with me joining the Sea Cadets and learning Morse code and semaphore. We would signal each other across the classroom and the teachers knew we were up to no good but hadn't got a scooby doo what we were messaging. Ha ha. Perkins, go and stand outside the classroom.

I used to nick off certain classes. Sometimes I would go down the woods and walk along the riverbank, other times I would go down to the main library in town and look through Janes Book of Fighting Ships. The authority on naval military might the world over. My Dad saw me a few times from his bus driving and challenged me but I mumbled some excuse or other and Mr Harris caught me in the library one day. We had an argument, in whispers....

Get back to school. What are you doing? I am revising the navy that I am going to join. Get back to school (all whispered) fuck off. Do you want to cause a scene? I don't mind but I don't think you are big enough to get me out of here and back to school so fuck off. So, he did. I got bollocked later.

It didn't help matters that all the kids from year before me could leave school at 15 and become apprentices or boy soldiers etc. but mine was the first year the minimum leaving age was lifted to 16. I had taken my initial tests to join the Navy in the Autumn of 1971 and the start of 1972 and passed what I needed to with flying colours, giving me the choice of careers of anything except for Artificer (didn't get all the maths questions right evidently) and just had to clear the medical.

The RN careers office was in Blackfriars Street, Salford. Just down from Market Street (long before the Arndale Centre was constructed). Lots of old buildings fronting onto a busy road. It's mainly pedestrianised these days. I just had to return for the medical. I had to take my spectacles with me for the eye test bit.

A very old- fashioned type of medical. Naked throughout. I had a thorough physical examination from a grumpy old doctor, which included him holding my balls and telling me to cough. Very demeaning.

So, I was proper on the back foot when he asked me to read the eye chart, just a blur to me. I spluttered that I couldn't and before I could say that my glasses were in their case, in my jacket, back in the bay I got changed in (didn't seem right to carry them naked, not sure why) and I didn't wear them at all unless I needed them.

He only heard I couldn't and shouted at me to get out and stop wasting his time. I was shuffled out by an assistant who told me that if I couldn't read the board, then I couldn't join the Navy. I was too shocked to speak and confused to say the least.

The walk and bus journey home was also a blur as all my career hopes and dreams had been completely trashed. I think I cried a bit. I probably cried a lot and felt pretty sorry for myself.

After explaining what happened to my parents, Dad was incensed and took up the cudgel by calling someone at the RN careers office and explaining that I hadn't been given a chance to use my prescription lenses to aid the eye test, as it was allowed. After a lengthy delay I was given another date for a medical and as agreed with Dad, I wore my glasses from the moment I left home until I got back after bussing into Manchester, walking to the careers office across the River Irwell into Salford and completing the medical.

I was offered a number of dates in 1974 to join up and selected December 3rd as the first date after a family camping holiday, my 17th birthday in September and a lad's holiday we had booked and paid for in early October. It had a nautical connection, of sorts. We hired a motor cruiser on the Norfolk Broads. Six teenagers, all aged sixteen / seventeen.

My last few months at school were a bind to be honest. I didn't study. I didn't give a shit. I was joining the Royal Navy. Not the attitude to take and one I would certainly advise my children and grandchildren not to mimic in any way but that is how it was.

It came as no surprise to me but did to my parents that I didn't get a pass in any of my GCE's, nor any suitable score in the subjects that I had taken to CSE. I think I tried hard on the day but without revision, there were great holes in my knowledge.

Chapter Ten

The Scallywag

Back on the estate in the early-70's, I had palled up with a different group of lads who went to other schools, partly by default and in order to explore the world with mates. We did some really stupid stuff. Mainly it was being chased by the bigger gangs, or occasionally when the odds were good, chasing them. I was the fastest runner in my year throughout junior and high school, so I could usually avoid most of the fights but when I had to stand my ground, then I would.

I wasn't particularly hard, I just got used to defending myself and retaliating first sometimes. I learned that getting the first punch in, often avoided getting a proper leathering, as it could shock others into inaction. Choose then to run or finish it off.

Our gang of five or six was really just a collection of social outcasts and gathered in mutual distaste of the rest. We got up to all sorts of wrong-doing... We were the "Other Guys"

One of our bases on rainy evenings was a bus shelter outside Stockport School on the A6. We would take up residence after buying a couple of bottles of cider then hurl abuse and the bottles at other groups or pairs of lads. Chase after them and fight. Sometimes we would "tank up" on cider then go out on manoeuvres. Chasing after youths, I could always catch them up and trip one or two and bring them down.

We couldn't go into the youth club in Dialstone Lane school as all our enemies would be in there and in big numbers, so every now and then we would all carry a couple of good sized pieces of aggregate and throw them in a quick barrage and put as many windows through in the area used for the disco and then leg it before anyone ran out after us.

Smashing big panes of glass can be quite gratifying when you feel that you are in a position of resistance. We put windows through on new build properties in Offerton and in Edgeley. We regularly tracked into Bridge Hall estate and around Adswood looking for trouble and usually found it.

Another fad we enjoyed was garden hopping. A lot of the posh houses in Offerton in the area surrounding Offerton Lane had privet hedges to divide the gardens. A lot had privets along the "fence line" onto the road. We would stand in a racing line on the opposite side of the road and then run full pelt into the hedge, turning it into a shoulder charge at the last minute, meant all your momentum was protected by your big coat and shoulder. Rather than crashing through, it sort of slowed you down as the hedge bent over with your weight and you could roll to your feet in one smooth move then run at the next hedge dividing the back gardens and go again, and again.

Seen from above it would have resembled something like the Grand National, though instead of horses it was just teenagers. Some of the hedges sprung back as they had been before, some were damaged beyond repair. Some had sneakily been grown next to chain link fencing which converted all the kinetic energy from charging at it into throwing you back on your arse. In those case's we had to find exit routes quickly and run up side paths or leap the fences by scrambling up them.

Being chased by angry adults and the police was all part of the fun and we used every ginnel (passageway) and short cut we could find to evade capture.

We also began going to Edgeley Park on a Friday night, not that I supported Stockport County, I had been a United fan all my life but Friday night was Fight Night.

The attendances were made up of City and United fans as well as County fans. The bonus of County playing on Friday nights was that it also drew the Saturday fans as well. We didn't as much fight each other but the away fans and in particular any club from Yorkshire or London.

In 1972 Stockport County drew West Ham United of the First Division in the League Cup after already beating Crystal Palace away. The Hammers fans were notorious for fighting and the match drew a big crowd, inside and outside of the ground. The fighting that night was enshrined into County's song based on the catchy Snoopy Vs The Red Baron tune.

They still sing it today...

> After the turn of the century
> In the clear blue skies over Edgeley
> Came a roaring and scoring that you've never heard
> When Stockport County scored their third
>
> Onto the field came the boys in blue
> They beat Palace and West Ham too
> West Ham tried and West Ham died
> Now they are buried together on the Popular Side
>
> Ten, twenty, thirty, forty, fifty or more
> The West Ham fans couldn't take any more
> We used our fists and we used our feet

And they ran like fuck down Castle Street

The fighting started from the moment the cockneys began arriving at the railway station. Continued throughout the game and when County won 2-1 it became carnage. I went with my "cousin" Ian Lowson, from Reddish. We had been childhood playmates when every adult seemed to be an aunt or an uncle and all the kids were classified as cousins. Not confusing at all.

Ian and I were in the thick of it on Castle Street and fought all the way from the football ground to the roundabout just outside the railway station. The police were making a valiant effort to maintain order, so it was all truncheons, whistles and flashing blue lights but they didn't make much in the way of inroads into stopping the fighting.

We avoided arrest. County had won. We had won. The victory was celebrated in the one pub we could get served in at the time, The George in Mersey Square where we met up and swapped stories over pints of cheap beer before getting the last bus back to the estate.

Dress code seemed to be of great importance in my youth. Winter-smart, was Crombie overcoats and we all wore "Parallels" brightly coloured baggy pants in a variety of colours. Mine were petrol blue.

Boots were the finishing item for the full outfit. My mates all wore Doc Martens, the true fashion item for the boot boys or bovver boys as we were all named by the tabloids. Summer dress code was denim jackets, denim pants held up by braces and Doc Martens. I couldn't afford to buy a pair and so used my hobnailed boots from cadets. They made a great crunching noise when walking along the road and quite useful for kicking people but totally hopeless in a chase....

We got caught by a bigger gang on Cale Green one evening in late 1973, or early 1974. That winter anyway. Three or four us and about a dozen of them, so we ran. I got about 50 yards when the hobnails under my leather soled boots turned me into a Crombie-coated version of Bambi on ice, so I had to turn and face them or be taken down from behind.

I couldn't see where the punches and kicks came from but I got knocked to the ground against a railing fence, sort of half sat, half lay when a lad swished something in front of my face backwards and forwards. A girl screamed. Then all the lads ran away and I lay with blood running from my nose and cuts around my eyes when a girl leaned in and asked where had Jesse slashed me... shit.

I climbed up and staggered away down Bramhall Lane with blood dripping down my face and caught up with my mates who had been hiding. I was in a bit of a daze and all I could say was that I had been slashed with a razor. However, upon closer inspection, the damage to my face had been caused by the punches and kicks. The razor had slashed right across the chest of my Crombie overcoat. Completely ruined it but my face was not going to be permanently scarred. Bonus.

I couldn't afford to buy a new Crombie. My Mum sewed it up as best she could but it was never the same. Shortly after I joined the Royal Navy later that year, she ditched it in the bin, along with some other of my bovver boy clothing. My jeans were used to patch up David's jeans and the hobnail boots didn't fit me anymore. The only relic of that time was my denim jacket and that went to sea with me.

That winter of 1973/74 seemed to be a never-ending run of parties as classmates were leaving for apprenticeships with Mirlees and Simons, plus some coming of age events for kids we were at cadets with. The routine was always similar, bring a bottle(s) and drink as much as you can. My mate Stan (David Stanton) got absolutely blootered at Karen Listers party on Cruttendon Road, Great Moor and as the party was breaking up and we were ordered home by Karen's Dad. Stan was sort of comatose sat on the wall.

We couldn't persuade him to stand up so I gave it a go to lift him up and grabbed both lapels of his denim jacket with both hands, gripping tight when Stan suddenly fell forward onto the floor face down. This sort of catapulted me over him, with my hands still embedded in his jacket, I landed chin first on the paving flags next to him knocked out.

Lots of blood and my chin was a mess. It is still scarred to this day. Mrs Lister patched me up with some wadding and plasters and we got going home. No matter of explaining would have my Mum believe that I hadn't been fighting....

At another event on the A6 in Heavily, we arrived with our bottle of whiskey and 2 cans of "Party 7" the 7-pint can invention by Mr Watney and when we went to stow them on the drinks cabinet realised that everyone else had brought shit or next to nothing, so we retreated from the living room and took up residence in the bathroom and locked the door to drink our stash privately. We had the sink full of cold water to keep the beer cool and only let people in when we thought it was okay.

At some point in the evening Kev Spencer got the shits and spent a long time sat on the bog. It didn't stop us drinking and we were determined to see off the whiskey and beer. Loz Wright got pissed really early and we stuffed him in the bath burbling while we continued to see off the booze. There was a mad knocking on the bathroom door, the girl who's party it was and her Dad were demanding we open the door, so I did.

In rushed the girl (who may be happy I cannot remember her name) and was holding a hand over her mouth and clearly wanted to throw up. Saw Kev on the bog, so turned to the bath, saw Loz curled up and the sink full of water and booze and so dived for the little gap between Kev's legs and threw up all over his thighs, cock and balls, whilst he was shouting and trying to stand up. Oh it was the funniest sight, never mind the smell of pooh and vomit! It took some cleaning up and then we were ordered out of the party... the march of shame down the stairs and into the cold outside....

Indoor recreational breaks were limited to Stockport Lads Club on Hempshaw Lane, in Offerton. I used to play football there, did a bit of boxing led by one of my mates big Jack Keeble who had been at a boxing club for donkeys years and gave us lots of advice. We also played snooker, did some work with weights and tried not to annoy the volunteers who staffed the club.

Back outside, we were invited by some remote friends of friends to join them in the regular Reddish versus Gorton gang fights and rendezvoused in a small industrial area on Station Road in Reddish. Strategically located across Mellands Playing Fields from Spurley Hey youth club on Mount Road.

The most disturbing sight was several crates of empty milk bottles being filled with petrol and rags, never mind the piles of half bricks and large bits of aggregate stone. Lessons on how to throw a petrol bomb without it pouring down your back and setting yourself on fire were being provided in what may have sufficed as a pre-event safety briefing or too- box talk.

The group of lads numbered well over 50 and once everyone was tooled up, we advanced across Mellands after climbing the fences in 3 groups. Seven or eight on each wing to act as guards and back up, with the main body heading straight for the point opposite the school but still inside Mellands fields fence. I was in the group on the left and had a perfect view as a massive barrage of bricks and petrol bombs were hurled at the school. Scary to say the least.

The assault ended when large groups of lads ran out of the school at the fence line and started to clamber over. The flames and sound of smashing glass was accompanied by sirens, as a couple of police cars and a van appeared, which resulted in someone shouting the standard warning "Scatter!" Police were also arriving from the Station Road side of Mellands and began wading into the gangs with truncheons, whistles, blue lights and sirens.

None of our little gang of visitors was caught as we dodged coppers, "Gorton-ites" and fleeing "Reddishers" and in the post-event debrief as we made our way back to Offerton, it was decided that we would leave our remote friends to fight their own battles in the future.... Watching the 1979 movie "The Warriors" with a fantastic sound-track brought back some of those gang fight memories.

Sometime in the summer of 1974, I took my little brother Ged out to kick a ball about on the "redgrar" (red-gravel) pitch near to "Wembley" the only grassed football pitch on the estate, other than a junior pitch in Offerton Hall Primary School, across the stream from Wembley. Mum suggested it would be a good opportunity to take the dog for a walk, so Lassie (on a lead) came with us.

Ged would be about four or five and it was just before I joined the Royal Navy. I would have been sixteen or so. There had been a series of tit-for-tat beatings between my sea cadet mates and the biggest gang on the estate. It had run over several weeks and I guess, they had the majority of wins. They came to school to seek out Steve Smith. We caught a few of them in the chippy near to cadets and bounced them about the A6 London Road, and so on.

My older cousins Steve and George Darlington, Steve Smith, me and a couple of others did a tour round the estate in George's car. Every time we saw a bunch of lads, we jumped out of the car and battered or chased and battered them over the course of an evening. Three or four fights including leathering seven or eight lads stood in the chippy. One at a time. It wasn't pretty. Most of them were shit scared of George who had just come out of the Army. So, we took full advantage.

It is Sunday morning and there is a game on Wembley, Offerton Social Club were playing someone. I knew that I wouldn't be welcome down on the grass pitch, so I played passing and trapping with Ged on the redgrar pitch and the dog mooched around us on the lead, which I stood on whilst I kicked the ball with my other foot. When a lad wearing the standard issue green parka coat road across the redgrar pitch towards me from the grass pitch, followed by half a dozen lads I knew.

I couldn't resort to rule number one when faced with those odds, to just run away as I had Ged and Lassie with me. So, I stood my ground and Ged stood beside me and held onto the dog lead with Lassie on the end. The scooter boy was Nick Seaton, who got off the bike and was a bit shorter than me, if a year or so older.

He faced me up and said "Someone tells me you were driving round the estate last night hitting some of my mates". Everyone is looking at me

"So?" I managed to muster

"So, someone might have to be taught a lesson" said the grinning Nick Seaton

"Are you going to hit him?" asked one of the entourage, could have been Robert Douglas who was a year younger than me

"I think so" said the smug Seaton, looking round at Douglas and starting to take his gloves off

I just thought I was going to get leathered so best get the first punch in, so launched a good one straight between his chin strap and the peak of his helmet. He went down like a sack of potatoes and I turned to face whoever was coming next, only to hear "It's a fair fight, one onto one, plus he has got his son with him" – not waiting for anything else I dived onto Seaton, pulled his helmet off to choke him with the strap and kept punching him in the face until someone hauled me off, saying "I think he's had enough" which was probably true. His face was a mess. I got up and offered him a chance to stand and fight again but he declined and I walked away with our Ged and the dog feeling just great. If a tad nervous when the adrenalin surge ended .....

For weeks I was threatened with an appearance from his big brother and his mates but it never materialised and I had no further mither with him.

However, a few of the wider gang came into Lipton's to threaten me when I was boning out a leg of pork. They told me they would be waiting outside the supermarket for when I finished work and I was going to get a battering. I jammed the knife into the wooden block and said okay. The first person to come anywhere near me was going to have the boning knife shoved in his belly. Then the stores assistant manager came over and ushered them out.

I cleaned the knife, made a sheath out of cardboard and taped it together and shoved the knife down the waistband of my pants. They weren't waiting for me but I kept the knife for a while until my Dad confiscated it, along with a flick knife I bought in Germany on a previous years school trip and a long steel dog chain I had as a belt. Never used in action but the flick knife was produced to prevent three lads from doing me on Lisburne Lane on my way home from cadets one night. The "click" as it flicked open was enough to stop them dead in their tracks. Job done.

My Dad gave me the boning knife back when I got married. It still sits in our cutlery drawer today. He also gave me the flick knife, which sits at the back of my sock drawer.

However, from working part-time as a Cutter in the Lipton's Supermarket butchers department, I went full-time from completing my O-Level examinations in the spring. It opened up a whole new environment for me. Customers. I had a lot of fun.

The butcher was a big fella called John C Allport. Taller than me and carrying far too much weight. He wasn't the nicest person, arrogant and really full of himself. I only got the job because his reputation scared off most other people who knew there was a vacancy. It was hard work as an assistant.

I had to "scrape" the cutting blocks off each night. Physically demanding, pushing a brush made of up metal blades and scouring the blood-soaked layer of wood off each night. Continually wiping the counters, brushing up, stocking up the chilled and frozen cabinets with joints, chickens, chops, making mince and completing sales.

Allport instructed me how to cut, how to weigh and how to price sales. The departments (butcher, greengrocer and provisions) didn't handle cash in Lipton's. Only the checkout team. We had to weigh and price the order, printing a sticky label off that got stuck on the bag and sealed it. All the prepared and sealed food in the chiller and frozen cabinets, was priced in the same way. We had to stocktake on a Saturday and account for everything, including the loose stuff like mince, chopped steak and kidney, chops etc. which remained on steel trays until a customer asked for a certain amount.

Allport also told me that no matter what the scheduled cost was (Allied Meats provided a price for all the raw materials, joints, full pigs, sides of beef etc.) we had to price up what we cut, prepared and weighed.

However, no matter what the scheduled cost of each item was on the scales, Allport instructed me to add a penny on every sale.

We were making over a thousand sales a week. He got a share in the "profits" when the department heads convened their divvy up on a Friday night and took out the difference between what should have been and what was. I don't profess to know any more than that as they kept that to themselves but one this is for sure, they were doing some sort of deal between them.

The rest of us who were privy to and part of the process, did not benefit from it. I did ask, just the once, what was in it for me and was told, I had a job. Be grateful. So, I used to take what I considered to be my share. Mum got a "wrap up" every week. Sometimes a joint, sometimes steak and kidney. She thought Allport was a good egg.

Little did she know I was stealing a small amount of something already stolen (in kind). £10 to £12 a week profit, if that is what they did, was a decent amount in 1974. To put into perspective, my wages were £11 a week.

I also played about with the penny put on a sale. If the customer was nice, I took it off. If they were nasty or miserable, I added it on. It must have played havoc with their weekly data. Ha ha.

Allport used to cut corners and do anything to save or make a penny. He had me make minced beef with all sorts of shit. Bits of fatty pork, liver to colour it up and push everything through the mincer twice, that way everything looked orange under the glow of the neon strip light strategically placed under the chiller counter.

I remember making some mince one day for a customer, she had sensibly bought a piece of stewing steak and watched me put it through the mincer and I automatically put it through a second time as per Allport's instructions.

The lady, challenged me on why I was putting it through twice and I had to quickly make up an excuse on the spot. "It's to iron out the air bubbles in the mince" and she just looked at me as I added "Little jets of air are inside the mincer helping it mince the beef, and you don't want too much air in your mince to you?" she carried on gawping at me, so I continued "Do you fry your mince before you put into a shepherds pie?" and she just nodded whilst still catching flies, so I went on "Well when you fry it, do you see it sort of sizzle and spit" and she nodded again. I said "There you go then, it's all the air escaping out of the little pieces of mince" as I bagged up her mince and slapped the price sticker on to seal it. "Mind how you go love, you don't want to be dropping that basket and having a nasty mince explosion..... next customer please?" as she carefully tiptoed off down between the produce aisles. Haha.

However, Allport's greatest gaffe was him talking to his big mate one day (I was at school so didn't actually see the event but it happened shortly before I arrived for my evening stint. His mate was bigger than Allport, so we must be talking eighteen stone plus and he had leant on the glass counter over the meat chiller, which promptly broke and shattered shards of glass all over the meat.

As I arrived Allport was rinsing glass off the joints of beef. He instructed me to continue washing the joints, as he carefully picked out the biggest pieces of glass and I was rinsing anything left. We got through all the beef, lamb and pork joints, then the chops. He turned round with a plate of steak and kidney and said to him that he must be joking but he just solemnly shook his head and shoved the tray of steak and kidney pieces to me to wash off, individually.

When I turned round he had two trays of mince and I point blank refused to handle it. He nearly cried when he threw it into the bone meal bin, where at least he would get a few pence per pound when the Smiths bone wagon arrived at closing time.... However, the fiasco didn't end there. By the time we got to Saturdays stock take and heavy clean, a lot of blood had dripped through the grille into the chiller along with fatty pieces of meat, bits of mince and other gunge, which had dried and hardened in the near freezing compartment.

Allport and I had many disagreements about the cleaning regime. His approach was to pour a bucketful of boiling water straight into the cabinet, let it soak in for a minute or two, then slosh it around with a scouring pad, them mop up the bloody mess and wring it back into the bucket. I always took a more measured approach based on keeping the water hot (in his, the water went almost immediately cold) and I attacked each hardy piece of dried blubber and blood systematically. My way was slightly slower than his but safer as you never know what was lurking in the goo, bits of bone for instance. Or in this case, pieces of glass...

Allport had made a start on scrubbing the block when he saw me, in his eyes, fannying about in the chiller compartment. So, he pushed me out of the way and told me to finish off the block instead. I dried my hands, got the scraping brush and started on the block. In the background I heard a big splosh as the contents of the bucket are emptied into the chiller compartment. Then a sloshing around as he did his usual. I heard him start to speak to another member of staff on the other side of the counter when he screamed like a girl.

I turned round to see that he had wrung a piece of glass into the palm of his hand and blood was pumping out over his hand and his greasy (was white) and bloody coverall. Then he fainted at the sight of blood. KARUMP. The member of staff on the other side looked at me and asked why I didn't catch him. I just shook my head. He trotted off to call an ambulance and I put a first aid dressing on his hand and applied pressure until the ambulance arrived.

Allport had come round by the time the ambulance arrived and was pretty pasty faced but told me to shut up the department at closing time. The usual routine was to carry on selling and put nothing away until the last customer left the supermarket, even if they weren't anywhere near the butchery. Not that night it didn't. I was packed away, cleaned up and shot out of the staff entrance at 5pm, complete with a nice (glass free) wrap up joint for my Mum.

We had a replacement manager for a week or two as Allport's gashed hand healed and the shop routines were quite casual until he returned to work.

Allport liked to catch me unawares. If I was at the block cutting up meat, he would sidle up behind me and start dry humping me against the block. Several times I picked up a steak knife and pressed it against his belly but it didn't seem to faze him and I had to dodge to avoid his hands groping my bum and privates on different occasions.

The ladies on the produce counter next to us were forever berating him and calling him queer, amongst many expletives. No-one had any political correctness barriers in those days. They just said it as it was. Not clever or pretty, just as it was.

I used to volunteer for the dinner time run to the chippy "Fiddlers" across the way on Lisburne Lane. It had several benefits for me. Time away from Allport being the main one. Cultivating the relationship with the ladies, as they controlled distribution of cheese and boiled ham at the produce counter being another.

I was hooked on little rolls of boiled ham or a slice of Cheshire cheese when I was working and they never said no. Although the produce section manager Tony did limit me to about half a pound of boiled ham and half a pound of Cheshire cheese a day.... The main reason I did the chippy run though, was the perks of taking the order into the chippy.

The chippy were always pleased with our custom as a dozen orders everyday must have helped with their turnover. The bonus was always a cuddle off Mrs Fidler and questions about how my Mum and Dad were from Charlie Fidler, as well as a treat while I waited. Do you want a pie or a fish today?

I would scoff one while wating for the complete order to be put together, then carry the load back over to the supermarket staff room, where the produce ladies would have a couple of slices of bread and butter waiting for me and a seat saved for me at the table, where I could eat my portion of fish and chips. They proper looked after me and I couldn't stop eating.

Autumn was a time for Allport to turn the screw on the meat providers, who traditionally increased the price of material in the run up to Christmas. Allport's routine was to buy boxes and boxes of big chickens (we were in the middle of a big council estate, Turkey wasn't affordable by all families and so chickens were cheap and always in demand then). Also he would buy an extra few full pigs. Cut off the legs and put them in the freezer with the pile of chickens. He would then instruct me to remove a certain number of pork legs to defrost overnight and ready for the demand the following day.

The chickens arrived and we formed a short chain from the back entrance, through produce, on to the butchers, into the massive walk-in fridge and on to the walk-in freezer at the back. It was always best to be in the chain away from the fridge. Allport didn't trust anyone, so had the Assistant Manager counting the number of cases off the back of the delivery van. The shelf-stockers in between, him at the fridge door, me at the freezer. The coldest and least sought after role. I would be freezing. Each crate of chickens was 30lb and came in thick cardboard boxes bound with iron wire.

We handled the crates by the wire. In the freezer it meant I had purple lines across my hands from the wire and the weight, along with "chill-blanes". Allport thought it was funny to throw the chicken crates at me, not to me. So I had to catch them. I threw one back at him and he lost his rag, grabbed me and pushed me into the freezer then pushed the door to. There was a little rod clipped inside the freezer, that could be pushed through a small hole and push against the freezer handle to escape but I looked and it wasn't there.

The bastard had already removed it and I guessed he had planned to shut me in the freezer at some point that day. I shouted to him to let me out but he just laughed. Piled up the remaining crates of chickens in the fridge, left and closed that door as well. The freezer and the fridge together were airtight and therefore sound proofed. I knew from previous experience. I guess he would have left me there a while to get really cold but I had other ideas.

I lit a fag and put my lighter up to smoke detector. Ha ha. All the fire alarms went off and he had to let me out as the store was evacuated. We exchanged punches on the way out through the back of the supermarket. I left him to explain things to the store manager and the Fire Service. I am sure he would have made sure I got the full blame.

The daily routine was to sell, sell, sell. Anything and everything we had in the run up to Christmas. Preparation for the following days activity would also be fitted in between selling and cleaning. One of them was how many frozen legs of pork to bring out of the deep freeze so they could defrost in the fridge. On one of the days Allport instructed me to lay out four legs of pork. I thought we would never sell four in a day so just got three out and left them in a big deep metal tray in the fridge.

Halfway through the following day I realised that we were getting through the pork quicker than I envisaged but was still confident we wouldn't but as a precaution, I would get a 4th leg of pork out of the freezer. I washed all the ice off under the hot tap and put it in the deep tray in the fridge, so it looked defrosted. It was getting towards closing time and we still had a couple of leg joints in the chiller display and thought I had got away with it.....

Despite Allport's sickly sweet selling skills, always calling ladies "Luvv"y and gents "Sir", in this case "Luvvy" wasn't having a joint from the chiller, she wanted a fresh one cutting. Moz, get the last leg out of the fridge, was the command. I knew he would know as soon as I placed it on the block as it made a thump rather than a plop. If he didn't then, he certainly did when he tried to slice through the skin and meat to the bone his knife hardly penetrated the frozen block of pork. If looks could kill, I would have been zapped like a laser and disintegrated on the spot.

Undeterred he picked up the 5lb cleaver, the biggest we had and launched an attack on the frozen lump. Thunk, chunk, chump and the sweat was pouring from his head as he tried to open up the prone leg. One of his big swings had got the cleaver really embedded in the bone of the leg and didn't come out when he lifted. Instead he tried to show off his strength by lifting the 5lb cleaver, complete with a 7lb or 8lb frozen leg of pork, like Arthur trying to withdraw Excalibur from the stone.

I looked on aghast as Allport had clearly instructed me never to lift a blade complete with a joint and try to smash my way through it as there was a huge risk of breaking your wrist. Those pesky physics things about weight, momentum and the transfer of the impact and dissipation of energy.

Clearly you are already reading ahead on this and you will not be surprised, as the couple buying the pork or I was, at the sound of Allport's wrist snapping when he thumped the leg and cleaver combination down onto the block. He squealed like a girl and fell to the floor clutching his wrist.

The Assistant Store Manager, Mr Booth, came and took him to Accident & Emergency in his car and I was left to (carefully) saw the bone and cut through the frozen pork to supply the subdued customer, then tidy up and close the butchers department so that I could leave dead on 5pm when the store shut. Another bonus day and a relief manager for a week. Allport returned complete with arm in plaster and directed operations and commanded sales whilst I did all the cutting, cleaning and preparation until the cast came off.

Reaching the age of 16 our attention was drawn to motorised travel, which in our case was going to be limited to a 50cc moped (a motorbike with pedals). Steve Smith bought a Yamaha FS1-E and Loz Wright a Honda SS50, both brand new. I dreamed of a Garelli Tiger Cross but couldn't afford a new one. However, opportunity often arrives in unexpected ways.

One of our neighbours, Mr Wild and his family were emigrating to Australia. Dad was interested in a tent and some camping stuff that Mr Wild was selling.

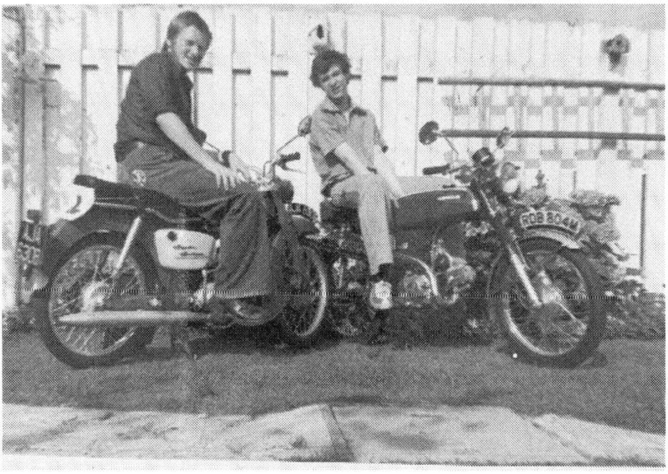

His council rented garage was right next to our house and I wandered over to see what Dad was buying and right at the back was a motorbike covered in a canvas sheet. What's that I enquired of Mr Wild. Oh, that's my old 50cc bike I used to race. Whoa. Now that perked up my attention. Can I have a look says I. You can have it if you want, responds Mr Wild.

Whoa. Opportunity. Let me get it running first said Mr Wild. Pop round to our house tomorrow.

The bike was a Honda 50cc motorbike. No pedals, therefore the legal age to ride it would be seventeen and I was still sixteen then. Mr Wild offered it to me for free. I said I couldn't and gave him a tenner. Dad didn't really understand motorbikes so I never bothered to explain the potential difficulties and went about my business of buying a helmet and painting the parts of the bike that had lain against the wall of Mr Wilds garage and had gone rusty. Though Dad did help me sort out the timing.

The bike was faster than my mate's new ones and whilst there's topped out at 40mph or so, mine would get up to 60mph, downhill, with the wind behind me. It also accelerated faster than theirs and I loved it. The cyclist who had ridden everywhere as a youngster now came out in me as a motorcyclist. We went all over the place and extended the range of pubs we went drinking in.

One favourite being the Crescent Arms in Disley (long gone now) we also biked all over the hills to exotic locations like New Mills, Hayfield and Whaley Bridge. Easy to get served walking into a pub carrying a bike helmet. No-one asked questions...

As you would imagine, I managed to get into trouble.

My first crash was on Dialstone Lane, Offerton, at the junction with Blackstone Road and not my fault.

A bus was paused in the road indicating to turn right into Blackstone with a car at the stop line on Blackstone indicating to turn right to come out. I was leading the three bikes in a column doing about 30mph and heading along Dialstone when the car came slowly out of Blackstone Road in front of the bus. We all braked but I was already too late as I realised I would hit the car / get crushed against the bus and tried to swerve behind the car and brake harder.

My foot pedal hit the kerb and that combined with the braking, flipped me down sideways into a slide, which ended when my wheels hit the other kerb and I was thrown onto the footpath and grass verge. I remember the bus driver shouting at the car driver and offering to get the police and an ambulance. I said that I was okay and didn't need the emergency services, I certainly didn't need the police for sure, nothing was broken and my cuts and bruises were just run of the mill. So, I climbed up and pushed my bike home.

Repairs were needed as the pedal was bent back and there was damage to handlebar and brake lever. I arranged to get the bike down to Howard & Sons, then on Great Portwood Street and agreed a price to repair them.

My next crash was quite epic. The three of us were on Turncroft Lane heading down to Newbridge Lane and I took the bad bend outside the entrance to Vernon and Woodbank parks too fast. I lay the bike as low as I could and braked but as I went round the bend could see the bike drifting over the centre line and caught a view of an approaching car and jammed the brakes fully on. This caused me to skid into the front of a Ford Anglia E-Type and went under it. Luckily the driver had seen me and was already braking. He had probably come to a halt as me and the bike slid under the front of his car.

My leg was trapped under the bike and I was yelling a lot. I looked up at the shocked looking driver, who was absolutely massive. He was the tallest bloke in Stockport and had both front seats removed in the Anglia and drove from sitting in the back seat. He was concerned that someone would blame him for his sitting position in the car but it was all my fault and said as much whilst apologising to him.

The police, fire service and ambulance all arrived pretty quickly and I was prized out. I didn't want the attention and had told Loz to get my bike out of the way and store it at his house, which wasn't far away and he did. Smithy gave me my helmet as I sat in the ambulance. No, I don't need to go to hospital. Yes, you do. So, I did. I got an invoice from them much later for £5 for emergency treatment for fucks sake. I didn't want to go.

After getting patched up at Accident & Emergency, I walked back to the scene to make sure my bike was out of the way and it was. However, the police were still there parked up in a panda car and as I passed trying to look as innocent as possible, the copper called out to me. I ignored him and pretended he was shouting to someone else when he said, you with the orange helmet. Oh, you mean me, right. So, he had me sat in the panda car and said he needed to see my paperwork. It's all at home I said, deploying the first line of defence. Right, says he, let's go and take a look then I can give you a lift.

So he taxied me to our house where the law abiding Mum and Dad were quick to invite him in and give him a cup of tea and began talking his head off, whilst I rooted around for my licence and certificate of insurance etc. Then gloomily sat there waiting for him to pick up the fact it was a motorbike and not a moped.

Our Mum and Dad never stop talking. It is to their credit that they can hold the attention of anyone, on any subject at any time, in any place. At home you are always offered a cup of tea and the biscuit box is produced. Never fails to provide the basis for a good natter.

It turned out the copper used to be in the Army and Dad is regaling stories of his time in the services and Mum has opened the biscuits to go with the brew. The outcome was a perfunctory glance at my documents by the copper as he was entertained and feted by the consummate hosts our parents are and I got away with it. Woo Hoo!

My continued evasion of the law was to come to an end when I got caught with a passenger on Newbridge Lane. I had picked up Bob Allison and was taking him home to the Emigration Pub on Newbridge Lane. We had been drinking in Offerton somewhere and the copper was sharp enough to understand it was a motorbike and not a moped.

I think the charges were riding a motorbike with no licence, no insurance (as it was invalidated by the offence), riding with an un-helmeted pillion passenger on L-plates. The drink riding offence didn't appear for whatever reason.

I was due to appear in the magistrates court on 3rd December 1974, the same day I had been given to join the Royal Navy. So, I pleaded guilty by letter and got a £10 fine and an endorsement. My Dad paid the fine and I paid him back when I got home for my first leave period. I sold the motorbike to Kev Spencer (who was now 17 and of legal age to ride it) for £80, so £70 went into my trusty Post Office savings account towards my holiday.

There was still time for one last hurrah with my mates when four of us (should have been six but two lads dropped out) hired a motor cruiser for a week on the Norfolk Broads. We all lied (to everyone) that we were 18 and competent to crew the boat, which we picked up in Stalham for a week of adventures. Jack Keeble, Bob Allison, Loz Wright and yours truly. October 1974.

The four of us held a planning meeting in Disley where Jack lived on a Saturday a week or two before we left for our holiday. Only Loz had a bike at this point and couldn't ferry the 3 of us on it, though we did consider it. We got a 192 bus to Hazel Grove and thumbed a lift up to Disley. People stopped for you in the old days. Now they wouldn't give a thought to picking up some teenagers, or anyone else for that matter.

We were having a good discussion on our pub crawl around Disley starting in our favourite pub The Crescent. We had missed the last bus back to anywhere and were contemplating thumbing it, less likely of a lift at that time of the night or walking the seven miles or so back home.

We got into the Rams Head, probably the biggest pub in Disley as our final stop and had aimed to have last orders in there but the landlady had just called "TIME" as we entered. Big Jack thinking quickly grabbed four empty pint pots off a table and acted like we had been in there all night and said we just want one more round before we go.

The landlady clearly not recognising Jack asked if we were from the function upstairs. Yes, said Jack confidently and she replied that that the bar upstairs was open for another hour. So up we trotted. Got served and noticed the half-eaten buffet for the 25th wedding anniversary party someone was having. So, we got stuck in and had a good supper of cheese, ham and egg-cress sandwiches, crisps and chicken drumsticks. Lovely.

We danced with some of the young ladies there, some of the Mum's and someone's Granny. They were all very welcoming and lovely. They even sorted us a lift out back to Stockport in a yellow Volkswagen Beetle. The couple in the front, Bob, Loz and me squeezed into the back.

The intention was to get dropped off at Nangreave Road in Heaviley, as a sort of equidistant spot for the 3 of us to then make our way home over the last mile or so in different directions. However, we had to stop early as Loz needed to throw up. He was never any good at holding his beer. So, after Loz had parted company with his share of the buffet, we got back on our way down Dialstone Lane when a police panda car opened up with its blue flashing lights and siren. So, we scattered.

Not a proper scatter as the three of us ran in the same direction, down Hillcrest Road where the panda car pulled us over. Two coppers got out and had us sit down against the fence. They wanted to know why we ran and we tried our best, whilst gasping and giggling, to explain that we were all under-age drinkers. One of the coppers was on the radio and I heard him ask for the description of the lad who had battered the police officer in Hazel Grove. What?

It got more worrying when two more cars and a van appeared and we were literally surrounded by a bunch of coppers when one of them points through the crowd at Bob and shouts "He's the one" and does no more than pull him up by the jacket and they drag him into the back of the van and start punching him.

I am trying to sober up like mad and understand what the hell is going on. Seemed a police officer had been attacked in Hazel Grove by a gang of lads, one of whom had a purple jacket on. Like the one that Bob was wearing. I explained we had been at a party in Disley in the Rams Head and got a lift off the couple in the yellow beetle, who must by now be somewhere in Heaton Moor on the A6.

It was only after the beetle had been stopped in Levenshulme and our story corroborated that they threw the battered and bleeding Bob out of the back of the van, immediately followed by a call on the radio that the lads had been discovered back in Hazel Grove. So, all the coppers, cars and vans shot off. Except for a sergeant who kneeled down and told us to forget all that had happened. He had our names and addresses and would follow it up with us if we tried anything on. No apology for the mistaken identity or anything. Then he left.

Bob was in a bit of a state, so Loz and me escorted him all the way home to the Emigration Pub on Newbridge Lane, Portwood. The scene of my motorbike arrest and we had to knock up his Mum and Dad, who were pretty livid to say the least. He and they, didn't follow it up and we logged it as a fact of life. All coppers are bastards... I know they are not and I have a lot of good friends who served but that night wasn't a good advert for them.

So on to our Norfolk Broads adventure. After getting a coach to Norwich and a bus out to Stalham, we had a briefing and were let loose with a valuable broads cruiser for an alcohol fuelled fun week.

We managed to steer the boat into some difficult situations and smashed one of the windows in the cockpit on a low bridge and snapped the little pennant mast at the front in a booze fuelled hilarious week. We all fell into the water at one point or another, caused havoc with other boat users and holidaymakers and got a bollocking for speeding up one waterway by a copper in a boat!

The last night was a bit of a haze and we spent up most of our money in a pub crawl around the four pubs in Stalham. Partly smarting from losing our deposit on the boat because of the damages and a large amount of beer tokens, we did get into a few scrapes with the locals and were physically thrown out of one pub after throwing darts into the wall instead of the board.

Not the cleverest of nights and we left it to the last thing to check the bus times the following morning and got it majestically wrong. By the time we caught the local bus into Norwich, we had missed our coach to Stockport. The next one was Sunday. Shit.

After a team consultation, Bob and Jack decided to thumb it home and headed off out of Norwich to find a junction and a sign saying North presumably. Loz and I decided to doss down in Norwich for the night.

We had enough money for some fish and chips and a couple of packets of fag's. We strolled around Norwich all day looking for a good place to doss down and chose the market. I rang my Dad with my last couple of 10 pence pieces, told him what happened and what our plans were for the night.

We returned to the market when it got dark and lay down on some canvas on a stall. That lasted all of half an hour as some security guards moved us on. We then selected a doorway and cuddled up as the temperatures fell. Smoking a fag every now and then to keep warm. As if. We had to keep a wary eye out for idiots still roaming the streets and growled at a couple of people who approached us. It was cold and very uncomfortable.

About 1am a panda car pulled up outside the shop and a copper shone a torch into our faces. "Maurice Perkins and Lawrence Wright" he questioned. We just sat there and nodded thinking Fucking Hell how did they know us. "Get in the car" so we did.

My Dad had driven down to Stockport police station on Lee Street and remonstrated with the duty sergeant that two sixteen-year old boys were dossing down in Norwich somewhere and he wanted the police to sort it out. The sergeant was sympathetic and they did a deal. My dad gave him a fiver. The sergeant called a counterpart in Norfolk police and said he would post the fiver through to him if they could get us picked up and put up overnight in a Bed & Breakfast. What a star.

It took the police all night to find us and when they did, good as gold, they arranged for us to spend the rest of it in a B&B. It was so lovely to be in a warm bed for the night and I fail to see the attraction of living on the streets unless all circumstances have been exhausted because it isn't nice.

We missed breakfast in the morning as we had to hot foot it across Norwich to get to the bus station for 9am, only we got the bus times mixed up again and found that the Sunday departure wasn't until noon.

So, we were tired and very hungry when we finally got home late Sunday evening.

It was only a matter of four more weeks or so and I would leave my civvie mates to their drinking and fighting to be trained in weapons handling and get a greater understanding of the Naval Discipline Act, which would slap me into shape like patting a block of butter. Probably...

Chapter Eleven

HMS Mercury

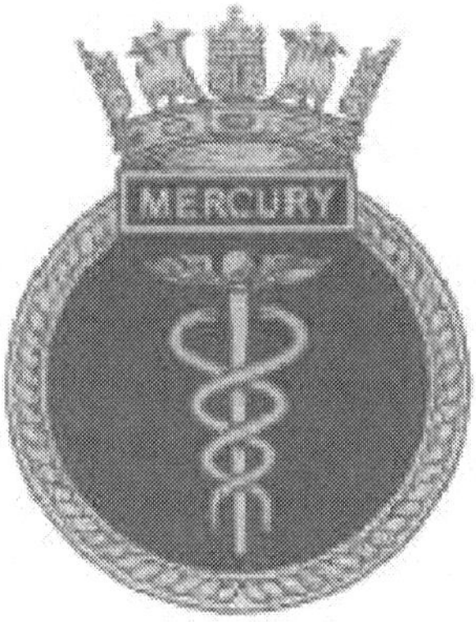

So, the teenage scallywag was now in the Royal Navy and having completed my basic training on the 2nd February 1975, had to head off for my professional training as a Radio Operator.

Radio school was a lot less authoritarian than basic training but we had to train for at least 2 weeks before any opportunity to get home on leave. First day after we paraded, we got the Mercury induction, which involved double time marching around the camp whilst the key buildings were pointed out and areas we were not supposed to enter etc.

We were each issued with a timetable. A bit like being back at school. Mine had TPX in amongst other things and I enquired with our Radio Supervisor (RS) instructor what that meant. He said its touch typing. I had a dickie fit and said I was here to be a radio operator not a typist. RS grabs Perkins by the ear and walks me over to a picture on the wall whilst he spelt out that radio operators needed to type messages into teleprinters not just write down Morse code. Ha, okay.

Touch typing is essentially a brainwashing exercise to learn where the keys are for each letter and function and be able to type without looking at the keyboard. A useful skill in the laptop and pc dominated world we would enjoy in the 80's forward. I could comfortably thump out sixty plus words a minute (60WPM)at 100% accuracy no problem by the time I left Mercury.

I already knew the Morse code and semaphore (which wasn't taught) but some kids could not get their heads around it. My challenge was to get my speed up from about twelve words per minute (WPM)to a minimum of eighteen words per minute, with an accuracy greater than 98%. So, the MRX classes were important. My best ever was 22WPM.

We got home that 3rd weekend and I can remember being with a bunch of classmates on the last train to Petersfield to pick up the RN buses that took us back to the camp. One of the boys was lamenting how hard it was to remember and understand the Morse code. He said he could only remember DAH DIT, the letter A. To which we all fell about laughing as that is the letter N. The letter A is DIT DAH, the opposite.

He branch-changed to Chef the following week. Hopefully he would be able to remember not to burn anything....

Mess raids were a continuing feature during training. With lads from other classes deploying fire hoses to soak clothing and bedding, chucking mattresses and bedding off the top bunks straight out into the gardens below, in the dry or rain, the sheets got dirty. It never stopped. There was always something. Sometimes they degenerated into proper fights until others eventually broke it up. Stand and be counted or curl up and cry. Most of us stood up.

Physical Training was a combination of many things. There was a well-worn cross-country course through the woods we had to do once a week. Football was a real pleasure, whether out on the grass pitches or indoors in the Drill Shed, or the Recreation Centre that had just been constructed.

Circuit training in the drill shed was another. I enjoyed keeping fit and made a good effort to improve on a number of areas to get my physical fitness up and generate some shape to my skinny frame.

We also did a bit of boxing down underneath one of the blocks, where a garage or store-room had been set up with some padded mats as a floor. No ring, just brick walls.

Whilst I had boxed as a youngster in cub scouts and in Stockport Lads Club, had a good understanding of avoiding being punched, I lacked the discipline to do it properly and would resort into scuffling. Sort of judo meets karate, meets Saturday afternoon wrestling and pure strangulation. Experience demonstrated to me that after a few punches are thrown, most fights degenerate into battles of the scuffler, as someone invariably jumps on your back or heads in for a clinch. He who scuffles best, generally comes out on top.

So, on a particular boxing session, which was a competition between two classes, I had been paired up with a lad from the other class called Hector. He was a bright lad if something of an eccentric. His mates asked me not to hurt him too much. I therefore adopted the full Marquis of Queensbury rules and maintained a good posture, jabbing him through his ineffective guard until one of my jabs put him down on the mats and he didn't get back up to resume the fight. A perfunctory win for our class, with no lasting harm to Hector. Everyone was satisfied.

The PTI obviously mistaking my theatrical boxing display for something akin to an afficionado, thought I would be good enough competition to fight with one of his boxing squad later that day. Thanks mate.

So, after classes had finished for the day, I duly returned to fight a lad who had been a junior boxing champion in his home county of Yorkshire. Not a particularly tough lad but clearly one who knew how to box and I didn't. My mates came along to cheer me on as I snaked out a couple of jabs and I began to feel my way into the fight but all fell silent as the boxer punched straight through my guard and knocked me out.

He was the first to get over me and apologise and help me get up. He must have thought I was going to get up and do him but it took all my effort to remember where I was and why I was lay on the floor..... no gum guard either, so my lips had a lovely bite imprint on the inside of my mouth above my lips which were sore for ages... cheers.

That was the last time I attempted to box anyone. I was a scrapper. Good at scuffling.

We continued with our radio training, voice, Morse code and typing. All getting faster and more accurate and shouted out at to make our handwriting neater to read. It's not okay to be able to read it yourself, quite often your messages were going to be handed to someone else to make critical decisions on and it had to be accurate and legible.

It is amazing how neat your writing will become under the threat of a slap round the head... As each week went by, there were those who fell by the wayside. Unable to maintain accuracy at speed, or failing to recite basic communications theory or by being a knob.

Those left made it through the basic radio operator training then we had to specialise. I had finished top of the class and got Captains prize for it. I chose the book "Sink the Bismark" and had it presented at Divisions. I still have it in my bookshelves.

So, to proceed into specialisation, we needed to complete a little form (the navy does love its forms) to indicate our preferences. At the time the Submarine Service had dibs on the top quartile of every course but I had absolutely no intention of going on one of those things.

The form looked a bit like this:

1st Choice	
2nd Choice	
3rd Choice	

With the nomenclature of Submarines (SM); General (G); or Tactical (T) to be inserted into the table. As I had finished top of the class, my form came with SM as first choice and I was left to indicate my 2nd or 3rd choices all by myself. I had already decided that I wasn't going underwater in any submarines for love nor money. No thank you sir.

I did no more than scribble out SM in the first choice box and put (G) in it. Then I put (T) in the second box. In the third box I wrote PVR which meant Premature Voluntary Release. As a junior sailor I could still give 2 weeks notice to leave the RN until I was 17 and a half. I scribbled a 4th choice box and wrote in SM. Then printed, signed my name and dated it, then submitted my form into the system.

The following day "PERKINS" came the shout when we were dossing about somewhere. I got marched in to see the officer in charge of training, who put me in the picture about the top quartile going into the submarine service. Not me I said. I want to be a Sparker (G) or a Bunting (T) but I would be a civilian before I went into a submarine.

The officer shouted that I could not hold the Navy to ransom. I responded that I wasn't holding the Navy to ransom. I wanted to be a Sparker, if not then a Bunting but I wasn't going in a submarine. This went on for some time but I was adamant. He had me marched out while he composed himself and made a decision.

I think the get out came because I was top of the class and it was deemed to be a reward for my efforts that my choice should be upheld. Probably saved face for someone somewhere. Who cares? I got placed on the Radio Operators (General) specialist training course. Where I finished top again and got another prize. Bonus. I was also a Class Leader all through basic radio training and my sparker training.

An unusual fact about the submarine service. No-one can join the Navy to go into submarines, you have to be selected. I saw it as a form of conscription. Years later I witnessed several people "avoiding the draft" to submarines, with the assistance of the scab-lifters. Feigning balance problems. Very few volunteered to go deep and smelly.

The one I witnessed went a little bit like this:

Vet: "Stand on one leg. Do you feel like you are going to fall over?"

Sailor: "No"

Vet: "Do you really want to join the submarine service?"

Sailor: "No"

Vet: "Stand on one leg. Do you feel like you are going to fall over (whilst nodding)?"

Sailor: "Ah" (getting it)" Yes"

Vet: "Good. No balance, no draft to submarines"

There were many rivalries in the services, between the army, navy and air-force. However, they also existed within the Naval services itself. The one between general service (Skimmers or Targets) and those of the submarine service (Deeps or Smellies) was a good one and wouldn't take much to light the blue touch paper of a scuffle here and there.

As a single person in the mob, I was entitled to four free travel warrants per year. In training they were allocated to Xmas, Easter and Summer leave, with one other as a spare. Any other journeys came out of my pocket. Not so bad if you lived in the south, not such a good thing if you lived in the regions. In my case, the north west. So, I hardly got home unless I paid for a seat in a car as far as someone would take you. One senior rate ran a car as far as Knutsford Services for a fiver, about a third of the train journey cost at the time. My Dad would meet us at Knutsford to take me home Friday night. We had to be at Knutsford at a specific time for the pick-up to journey back down to Mercury. I could only afford even that only now and then. Money was tight in training.

Not getting home enough was getting me down and I am not ashamed to say I was homesick. Properly so. Mercury is out of the way up in the Hampshire Downs. A beautiful part of the world but two and half miles to the nearest village of Clanfield and eight or nine miles from Petersfield, where there was a railway station.

I remember talking at length to my instructor about the homesickness and desire to hand in my notice and leave. So, with the training officer's permission, I was granted a compassionate warrant and went home to speak to my parents about it.

Dad thought it would be the wrong move to come out of the forces. Unemployment in 1975 in the UK was high as the country had gone into economic stagnation as part of a recession. Not a good time to be a civvy he said. So, I went back and made the decision to remain in the mob. The training officer and my instructor both backed my decision and determined that I would have a great career in the navy.

Coming up for Easter Leave in 1975 the wintry weather really hit the south of England, with blizzards and drifting snow forecast. For us in training it meant an early set off home. We got an additional couple of days before we should have. Then a good week or two at home before returning for the final set of exams to qualify as a Junior Radio Operator (G).

Coming back from Easter Leave we had about fifteen lads in a compartment for six. Some trains were full of little boxed compartments in the 70's and the trains were known as "slam door" rolling stock. Doors were not connected into the trains brake loop like they are today, probably after a number of incidents involving people falling or being thrown out of trains. We didn't know all that then of course, this was just an opportunity to play.

One of the boys was asleep in the window seat with his legs up on the window ledge on the other side of the door. Someone thought it would be a good idea to open the door as we thundered south from London to shit him up. Which it did.

The door hinged back from our direction of travel and opened with a bang. He woke up and shouted in alarm. Cue the rest of us falling about laughing our heads off as the sound of tracks and the inrushing air created a racket. Then we had to close the door. That was an effort.

So, two lads are leaning out of the doorway holding the door edge. Four or five boys are holding them in the train by their belts and holding onto them. A few of us are stood up with the window slide down pushing with all our might. Another one of those physics thingies again, where the maths on the weight of the door against the onrushing air from the trains speed all combine to make the door weigh about ten times its real weight as we attempt to manhandle it closed. But we do. It closes with a thump and everyone sits down except for me. I am still stood up with my fingers trapped in the closed hinge of the door.

Guys, we need to open the door again I think I calmly said (it wasn't hurting at that moment in time). Yeh, yes Moz of course it is. It is I said, then I shouted at them to open the fucking door as my fingers were starting to hurt. Someone said yes, his fingers are trapped so the door was opened. I pull my hand in and blood starts spurting out of the ends of two of my fingers and the nails are broken.

Cue howls of protest as people try to dodge the spraying blood whilst also not falling out of the door which had thumped open again, with the resulting in-rush of air and extra noise. I jammed a cotton hanky (I used to have them in those days) over my hand as the rest of the boys began the same task to get the door closed again. Which they did.

I lost the nails on two fingers and they were very sore for a long time and nearly stopped me taking part in the Brickwood's Junior Field Gun competition. I had auditioned along with virtually every other member of the camp who was fit enough. Whether junior trainee's, ships company and other courses taking place. The only stipulation was we had to be junior rates.

The PTI's ran a series of tests, which included lifting and carrying one of the wheels (which weighed more than me). Running a circuit of the camp to a stopwatch and a series of standing jumps. The applicants were whittled down to the bunch photographed on the next page.

The Junior Field Gun used the same gun and limber as the "professionals" used at the Royal Tournament and in the annual competition between the various naval commands. We just didn't go over any obstacles. We had to run the gun and limber. Take them apart. Rebuild and fire 3 rounds, then a sprint finish the length of the course.

We had a six-week training period where we drilled with the gun and limber after classes and in our own time every day. We also completed a two-mile run every morning and carried out circuit training in the drill shed at lunchtime. The field gun team also had tables set aside for us at all meal-times and we had to drink three pints of milk a day and eat at least 2lbs of meat and or half a dozen eggs for the protein, every day. I was probably at my fittest in the six years I served in the navy at that time. I also bulked out a bit.

There was a one-day tournament, sponsored by Brickwood's Brewery, and held at HMS Collingwood, in Fareham. Every training camp in Portsmouth entered teams. Mercury had an A and a B team. I made wheel number in the B Team. We also appeared and displayed at a number of summer fetes in 1975.

Excitement built as we neared the end of our training. Final Divisions and presenting of course awards and the sea drafts we all craved for. I was disappointed as hell to lose out on a sea draft straight out of training and was instead posted to the not so secret, secret bunker in Northwood, North London, not far from Watford. It was an experience. Not as good as being at sea but eventful none the less. I was posted there with a lad called Dale Reynolds.

I remember in training and we were all wrestling with our nicknames. Polly in my case and Dale wanted to be called Burt, as in Burt Reynolds but someone in the mess said, more like Debbie than Burt. But I don't like Debbie said Dale, which was the worst thing he could have said. He became Debbie and it stayed that way for ever.

Chapter Twelve

HMS Warrior

Debbie and Polly took the service warrant down to HMS Warrior. Northwood (along with Whitehall) provided the Royal Navy with a centralised communications facility far underground (and possibly safe) in its nuclear resistant bunkers in London.

Friday was the travel day, we left Mercury sometime in the morning and had a lunchtime in London before getting the Tube out to Northwood and a taxi to the gatehouse.

Going down the bunkers was referred to as "Going down the hole" as we entered the catacomb of corridors, operations rooms, communication centres, meeting rooms, hundreds of bunk beds and a large number of galleys (kitchens), toilets, showers and bathrooms for when longer stays would be required in the event of a nuclear war.

We were both assigned to D watch (shift) down the hole. Working an 8-day roster that went as follows:

- Day 1 was 1230-1930
- Day 2 was 0730-1230 and 1930-0730
- Day 3 was a Rest Day
- Day 4 was 1230-1930
- Day 5 was 0730-1230 and 1930-0730
- Day 6 was a Rest Day
- Day 7 was a Rest Day
- Day 8 was a Rest Day

Following the induction, we set to on the first day of our 8-day roster, an afternoon. I was introduced to the D-Watch Radio Supervisor, Tony Amato but didn't click until I saw the watch list. We all had a number by which to identify us and with which we signed for the receipt of signals etc. D1 was T.Amato and like a fool said, "Tomato" at which point Tony Amato punched me in the side of the head. "RS to you sprog" he grunted.

Tamato was an alcoholic. Many that I served with were tolerated in the 70's under the rule that as long as you could turn to for your duty, even smelling of booze, then the Navy let you get on with things. It was only when you couldn't do your job was any form of intervention made. Usually a drying out course at the Navy's hospital base RNH Haslar or the tri-service looney bin at Netley, near Southampton.

The afternoon wasn't bad. The following day was a culture shock. A forenoon followed by a 12-hour night shift. I struggled to stay awake that night and actually fell asleep on a teleprinter buzzing and shaking its signals out with me asleep on the casing, bent at the waist. I was like death warmed up going for breakfast on Day 3, our Rest Day. Don't waste it was the cry and we will see you at lunchtime in the Galaxy Club, the NAAFI bar in the middle of the base.

8-day rosters pay no respects to the proper days of the week. It was actually a Sunday and after one in the Club we made our way out onto the big council estate of South Oxhey where there were numerous pubs. We were getting near to closing time and I was thinking that's not bad, when the guys all drained their glasses and said they were off to Holy Joes. Grab a taxi and see us there.

Now you cannot always tell what is genuine and what is a wind up in the Navy but Debbie and I dutifully got outside into a taxi and tentatively asked the driver to take us to Holy Joes. No problem he said and tore off down the road to drop us off at St. Joseph and the Apostles Roman Catholic Church Social Club for all day drinking on a Sunday! I think we had to pay 20p or something and sign in as visitors but they loved us in there because we drank loads and never caused any trouble.

As a sprog, it was our job to maintain the "broadcasts" the four printers that churned out all the signals for all the officers, teams and parts of the

RN command. Each signal was accompanied by a tape that printed out from a separate port, of that signal in Murray Code format. A series of holes and spaces for each letter, number of special characters.

Our role as a sprog was to "receive" it on behalf of the command by tearing it off the printer roll, attaching the also separated Murray code tape fancily formed into a figure of eight (for easy transmission onwards) and stapled to the corner of the signal. Write down the time of receipt and your own individual watch ID and place it into a tray.

Routers were responsible for the onward internal transfer of those signals. Some went into vacuum tubes that whooshed along the corridors to thump home in a basket somewhere inside the underground citadel. Some were assigned to small mounds in trays to be re-sent down particular routes to specific locations and other communications centres around the UK and the rest of the globe. After a while, it became a hobby to be able to read the Murray Code, which was helpful to know immediately where to tear it off from the next one.

Working the broadcast bays was a bind. Four teleprinters continually spewing out messages 24/7. The volume tended to decrease around 01:00 hrs until about 06:00 hrs before firing up again and working as hard as a busy chip shop on a Friday night.

Once I got my mojo right, the nightshifts weren't always bad. Some of us would be detailed to collect our night victuals from the cookhouse. A couple of boxes of stuff. Often big bags of bacon, sausages and eggs, with catering sized cans of beans. Sometimes there would be some nice stuff that may had been destined for the wardroom, like cakes and buns but mainly it was stuff we could easily cook up down the hole.

During the nightshift, we all got an hour off. Tamato staggered the watch, so that every group had a sprog (like me) in it. Your one hour was enough time to get up and out of the hole, past the Royal Marine (bootneck) security guards and over to the NAAFI Club, the Galaxy for a couple of pints, then wind your way back down the hole to relieve whoever was going next. The watch started at 19:30 and groups were let out for 1 hour at 20:00, 21:00 and 22:00 each night we worked.

Tamato gave cash to one of the sprogs in each group. They had to buy a can of coke and two glasses of rum. Pour out half of the coke and fill with the 2 rums. Drink your own drinks then carry the opened can of coke back down the hole. A spotty faced youth with a can of coke in his hand must have looked innocent. If the boatneck's had known, we would have been in the shit, full and proper. However, boatneck's were not necessarily recruited for their intelligence and none of us ever got caught.

So Tamato would take the last hour and go into the Senior Rates bar for his fix, along with three double rum and cokes that he would have in the fridge down the hole. He generally fell asleep after the feast at 01:00 hours after most of the radio traffic stopped or slowed down and be roused for a wash before he handed over the watch at 07:30.

Tamato moved on and we got a new RS. I cannot remember his name but I nicknamed him The Walrus as he had black nasal hair that came out of his nostrils and curled up either side of his nose like small black tusks. It was horrible. Whenever I was in front of him I thought how awful it made his already ugly mug look. His sidekick was a killick (Leading Radio Operator) called Ken Middlecoate, who was a cunt.

He liked to tease the wrens and one girl in particular. He would work in tandem with a scouse Able Rate. One of them would get her talking and the other would ram a paper gash sack over her head and then staple it to the hem of her skirt so that when she tried to push the bag off it would lift up her dress and show all her smalls. Lovely guys. Both heavy drinkers.

My first run in with them was in the first week or so drinking with Middlecoate and the Scouser. I was paralytic in the Galaxy Club and when Middlecoate bought a round I said I couldn't drink anymore. He faced up to me said I was disrespecting him, he had bought me a beer and expected me to either drink it or we would have to have a fight outside.

I can remember thinking if I drank anymore I would likely throw up so thought a fight won't be half as bad. We stumbled outside and Middlecoate hit me with a gut shot before I could even face up properly. I sank to the floor and promptly threw up. Everyone laughed and went back inside the club.

Middlecoate and The Walrus got me good style when we moved to the comcen (Communications Centre) behind the operations room for a big exercise. We were spaced along and around and L-shaped annexe with bits of kit and odd communications links dotted about and shoved into alcoves but we were organised into a system and got on with it.

The Walrus called me over and said go tell Middlecoate that all that traffic (big pile of signals) has to be sent to Pompey (Portsmouth) by midnight. Aye, aye POTS (the old title for a Radio Supervisor, of Petty Officer Telegraphist) and walked round the corner to Middlecoate. Ken, the RS said that all that traffic has to get to Pompey by midnight. He just carried on bashing away on the keyboard of an engineering link composing a message and ignored me. I was stood right next to him, he must have heard me but I repeated the message. No response. I looked over my shoulder and all four broadcast bays were churning out messages, which I was going to have to separate and log in but I repeated myself a third time and then headed over to the broadcast bays to sort out the paper mountains on the floor.

A little after midnight The Walrus lets out a roar and screams at Middlecoate, why haven't all those signals been sent to Pompey, they are closing down at midnight and wanted them all in by then. Middlecoate just shakes his head and said that no-one had mentioned it. "Perkins!" was the next shout and I scurried over to form a little trio. Walrus screams I told you to tell Middlecoate that all that traffic had to get to Pompey by midnight. I know, I stammered and looked at Middlecoate then the Walrus, saying that I had told him, I was stood right next to him. THWAK !

Middlecoate punched me in the side of the head and knocked me to the floor. As he stood over me he shouted "Did I say yes? Did I nod my head? Did I acknowledge your message in any way? All I could do was shake my head, as Middlecoate repeated the lesson "Always make sure you get receipt of a message"

It was a hard and painful lesson and one I have never forgotten. Don't make assumptions. Remember the word ASSUME contains three key elements don't make an ASS out of U and ME. So, assume nothing. Make sure.

Manchester United had been relegated to the then Second Division at the end of the 1973/74 season. Promptly won the Second Division and had bounced back and were doing well in the 1975/76 season. Every now and then, the railways would run a cheap ticket offer and when I saw the £5 day return decided to get to the game versus Sheffield United on 23rd August.

All went to plan pretty much, bus from Warrior to Watford, early train from Watford to Stockport and it was full of "Cockney Reds" singing away and drinking, so I joined in with them. Jumped off the train at Stockport and met some of my mates for a few beers before getting back on another train, changing at Oxford Road and on into the Old Trafford Halt.

It was a great game that MUFC won at a canter. I was bouncing up and down in the Stretford End and didn't notice someone steal my wallet out of my jeans pocket at the back. I have always (uncomfortably) shoved my wallet into my jeans front pocket after this incident.

As the game drew to a close and I reached for my wallet to go and buy some beers, it was then that I noticed it had gone. I shouted out around me to the departing crowd that I needed my RN I.D. card back and my train ticket at least. Someone found my wallet (empty), my ID card rolled up from a different direction and my Post Office bank book which had £5 in it. Everything else had gone. Shit.

I needed to get home and borrow some money from Mum and Dad, only I hadn't told them I would be home, as it was never part of the plan. In and out and back to Watford for a Sunday drink with mates and a Monday afternoon watch down the hole. So, I switched into contingency planning.

I had to bundle myself in the middle of the swarm of United fans at the Halt and got onto the train without a ticket. There was only crowd control at Oxford Road, no ticket check and exited Stockport station in a swarm again flashing a cigarette case at the harassed looking staff and walked home.

I can still remember the look of shock on Mum and Dad's faces as they were washing and drying the pots from tea as I strolled through the back garden gate. "Didn't you get my letter?" was my initial foray into explaining myself.... I asked Dad for a borrow but he was brassic.

I had some coins but not enough for the single fare from Stockport to Watford, which was £9 something. We didn't want to knock on doors asking for money off anyone else and then I remembered a briefing given at some point in my training that if all else failed, go to a police station where a travel warrant back to base would be provided.

So, Dad drove us to Lee Street police station. The Stockport HQ and I asked the kindly looking policewoman on the front desk for a military travel warrant, after explaining that I had been robbed. She was in the process of telling me to do one when a sergeant got up and told her to hang on. He had been on an admin course at some point and seemed to remember something about military warrants.

He stood on a chair and got a big book covered in dust from a shelf high up, blew the dust off it and opened it up. It contained guidance and a sheaf of military warrants. With further guidance of how the police would recover their costs against the military for any other sundry items. It did include cash for sundry item's so I asked for a fiver and got it.

I stayed overnight with Mum, Dad, David and Ged watching the telly and catching up on things. Sunday was a travelling day and I had fiver for beer chits. Hey. I met up with Stanton and Spencer and we had a few beers in a pub outside the railway station, then I bought a carry out and got on the last train that would get me to Watford.

Drinking the remaining beers, I must have fallen asleep with my feet up when I felt the train lurch and heard the public address system say Watford. So, I opened the door (still good old slam door rolling stock) and threw myself onto the platform which had a sign on it saying Nuneaton. Shit. So, I jumped back in the train and slammed the door as the guard and platform staff were sounding whistles and the train, which had started to move off, slammed its brakes on. I think I mumbled an apology to the guard and got back to sleep again.

The train set off and continued our journey. I woke from a heavy sleep to see the train slowly starting to move out of Watford station so I re-enacted my Nuneaton performance by throwing myself out of a moving train, which isn't the cleverest thing to do when you are a) pissed and b) disorientated from being half asleep and tumbled along the platform for a short distance before I heard whistles and brakes as the train slammed its brakes on again.

This time the platform staff and guard were less than impressed and I can remember threatening them all with degrees of violence if they touched me. I must have done enough because they all stood off and I half-limped and walked out of the station where I gathered my wits. I checked my pocket for my wallet and ID card. Check. I counted out how much money I had. 55 pence.

Too late for a bus, it would have to be a taxi. I knew it cost a lot more than 55 pence from Watford railway station to HMS Warrior at Northwood but I thought I could go as far as 55 pence on the clock of the taxi and walk the remainder after obtaining suitable directions. This was my Plan A and it didn't survive the Watford circular expressway, which wasn't suitable for pedestrians, as the clock turned into a quid and I hadn't got a clue where I was.

Plan B was therefore quickly formulated and would consist of a candid explanation to the taxi driver, once we reached the gatehouse. I was sure he would take an IOU and I could sort things out the following day. Which is sort of what happened, except it didn't include the taxi driver blowing his top and insisting that the gatehouse oversee the signing of an IOU, with him and them (brilliant because they put it into their logbook and I knew there would be a penance for it) and validating who I was and crucially, that I had the means to pay. It was a blank week but I did have a post office book with £5 in it.

I owed the taxi driver £3. I had to get a bus from the main gate the following morning into Watford. Draw out the whole fiver from my Post Office account. Make my way to the railway station and wait for the taxi driver, who I then paid the £3 to (no tip as I would have preferred to keep my indiscretion under the radar of the Warrant Officer), before getting another bus back to Northwood. I think I had about a quid to last me until pay day on the Thursday. I just had enough time to get changed, have a bite to eat and get down the hole for my afternoon.

Sure enough, as I signed in, Tamato informed me that I needed to pop down to the Fleet Chief Radio Supervisors office (the Warrant Officer) who had me explain my tale, without any mention of jumping out of moving trains of course and he gave me a bollocking. Thank you Sir. Now back to work lad and stay out of trouble.

The Fleet Chief promoted me on the 19th January 1976 to acting RO1 (Radio Operator first class) on account that I was now 18 (overdue from September when it was my birthday) and no longer a junior. It was nice and I got a couple of quid extra a fortnight but would become a burden when I did get to sea when I joined the Antrim in April 1976 along with my oppo Debbie Reynolds. Seemed we were destined to spend time together.

Chapter Thirteen

HMS Antrim

Finally getting a sea draft, acting/RO1 Moz Perkins joins HMS Antrim in April 1976 and served on there until May 1978. Two hugely influential (in terms of my development) and very eventful years.

First day as an acting/RO1, I was despatched down to the CCR (Communications Control Room) the heart of all that was needed to tune radios and remote link them to wherever they needed to be used. The bridge, the ops room, etc. but I couldn't do anything, I didn't know how. George Bullyment our Radio Supervisor said I needed to smarten up quick, he couldn't have an RO1 in his complement that couldn't pull his weight.

So, I commenced an intense period of learning. Dave Pristaw was the senior AB in my watch and he taught me a lot but I also doubled up and spent a lot of my own time with the senior AB on the opposite watch, Billy Lounton, a gritty and no-nonsense Geordie. I was a fast learner and between them they got me so up to speed so that I could work at their level within a couple of months. I got a lot of stick in the early weeks but my willingness to get stuck in with my own time helped bridge a lot of difficult situations.

There was a lot of piss taking as well. Naval personnel take great delight in winding up colleagues and others and will undertake it mercilessly and incessantly.

During my first week of initiation into all that was good, funny and bad George Bullyment instructed me to float test the Stornophone batteries on his desk. You can do that as an Acting RO1 can't you he challenged. So, I grabbed the pile of batteries from him and started to test them by shoving them into the tester and watching the little meter register how much charge they had.

I put the battery in one way, then the other and the little needle remained still, as if attached to the bottom of the meter. I tried another one as the sniggers started, then another until the whole MCO (Main Communications Office) had erupted into guffaws of laughter at my predicament until George walked over, grabbed all the batteries in one hand and pinched my ear with his other and said come with me.

We walked up the passageway past the wheelhouse, where a couple of them stuck their heads out and laughed as George dragged me along by one ear to the ladder up to the forecastle (pointy end at the front of the ship) and as the ship ploughed along he threw one battery into the sea and said "that one doesn't float" and the same again as he threw all the batteries one at a time into the sea. Ah, float test meant throw overboard... Lesson number 1. There would be many, many more.

Our Chief Radio Supervisor, CRS Dave Eggars, also known as "Snake Eyes" had a wonderful method of raising a working party when all resources were utilised or on watch. He would have a small line of "jankers" people who had done wrong or who he had caught out when he questioned why someone was doing something that he didn't like. He called them his "Just" ratings.

His approach was based on a series of quick-fire questions, a bit like the "Gong Show" however, in the television show it was all about providing answers without using the words Yes or No. In Snake Eyes world it was the word "Just" and he called them (us) "Just" ratings. He hated them. If he caught you doing something he would get up close and stare into your eyes asking quick fire questions along the lines of "What are you doing? Why aren't you doing something else?" and if you could answer him without using the word Just, then you kind of got away with it.

He would say that using JUST as part of your excuse was child-like defensive behaviour because you had been caught doing something wrong, which he probably didn't know about and therefore testament to him, to find you doing something wrong and trying to squeeze out a reasoning that was in fact based on a load of bollocks.

It is really hard when put under pressure, to provide reasoning for your activity when you have been caught out. Try it. Snake Eyes would gather a few "Just" ratings together for additional work outside of watches and normal working hours and technically not part of a punishment detail (under the Naval Discipline Act) and it was hard to avoid.

Other than my professional development as a radio operator, we also had "part of ship" duties, which translates to every department / team within the ship, is responsible for part of it in terms of maintenance. Maintenance equated to two simple rules really, if it moves grease it, if it doesn't then paint it. Ours was the bridge, flagdeck, forward mast and forward funnel, plus the messdeck and "flats" bits of passageway connecting different parts of the ship, around the messdeck.

Flats needed brushing and polishing, the compartment walls and screens needed painting. The flats needed the polish stripping, the tiles scrubbing and then laying new polish again. Any hint of paint bubbling on the exterior was an immediate chip off and re-paint in the constant battle against the corrosion of salt water.

Remembering to put down the essential layers after chipping down to bare metal, of a coat of lead oxide (red lead), which dried quickly enabling the first of two layers of "undercoat2 to be painted on and finally, two layers of "topcoat".

Our life at sea was dominated by the need to polish and paint, whilst we concocted as many reasons not to polish and paint as was humanly possible. It was a bind.

Loafing about on the flag deck with a fag in one hand and a paint brush in the other was a Buntings wet dream when it came to maintenance. Whilst Sparkers hated polishing the passageway outside the MCO and critically just above Snake Eyes office as it clearly put you in the firing line for his "Just Rating" attacks.

In June 1976, I was invited to the King of Sweden's wedding.

When I say that I was invited, it wasn't a personal invitation as such. King Carl Gustaf being a navy man had requested a royal guard made up of the Navies of the United Kingdom, Norway, Finland, Denmark and Sweden. A rather grand affair.

I don't recall being asked to be part of the royal guard, I think it was more like I was detailed. Anyway, we drilled for weeks either on board on the flight deck or on the jetty when we were alongside.

The rifle of choice in the 70's was the trusty L1A1 Self Loading Rifle, 7.62mm known affectionately in the mob as the SLR and it weighed about 10lbs. The gun I was nearly a marksman with.

The drills were repetitive. We had our Number 1's (best bib and tucker) dry cleaned and ironed. Boots were polished so they gleamed. Webbing was whitened, re-whitened, wee-whitened. It was a never-ending cycle of activity but by the time we arrived in Stockholm in blindingly good weather, we looked bloody good.

I almost missed it as an all-day drinking binge and late-night chippy run almost ended in disaster when we got jumped outside the chip shop on Queens Street in the area of Pompey known as Portsea by a large gang of civilian boot boys. There were only three of us and about fifteen or twenty of them and they had bracketed us against the line of shops that used to be there.

Surrounded, we decided to charge them. I had my darts in my pocket and shoved them through the knuckles of one hand, my matelot mate had a big clasp knife opened with a blade on one side and a marlin spike on the other. Using those, we got away lightly but the civvy, Bob Allison visiting from Worthing, ended up with a broken jaw and lost some teeth I think. I dislocated two fingers on my left hand when I grabbed a lad by the jacket and he slid over and down.

Luckily for us, Royal Naval Regulators were on the scene from HMS Nelson pretty quickly, then the police arrived and the civvie thugs scattered. Otherwise I think we would have been more seriously hurt. Whilst we were being interviewed by the Regulators and Hampshire Constabulary, we heard on their radios of two other sailors being stabbed in Portsea.

After a visit to Accident & Emergency, where we left Bob, as he had serious dental damage and my fingers had been re-located (pulled out) and strapped up. I missed about a week of drills and got some light cleaning duties but as it was my left hand, it had less to do in the chucking about of the SLR to come to attention, present arms or stand easy. So, I didn't get thrown out of the party.

The body of circa 120 spick and span Antrim men were carefully deposited shoreside and we marched around past the palace and took up a position on the road across the water from the palace. Other ships companies representing the Nordic navies formed up around us. I can remember us whispering comments to those alongside us at how scruffy the other mobs looked. They had long hair, some had moustaches (banned in the RN unless it all joined up around your head as a full set) and just not as sharp and crisp as us.

We didn't get to see the wedding of course but were there to present arms and represent the United Kingdom as King Gustav and Queen Silvia trotted past in a picturesque coach and horses. All pomp and circumstance. After they and the accompanying horse guards had departed the road, all the navy contingents needed to shoulder arms and march behind the royal party.

The Finnish navy were just in front of us and they were already looking perturbed as the Swedish and Norwegian navy contingents had danced and dodged around the mounds of shit dropped by some of the hundreds of horses that preceded us and began to do the same.

The officer in charge, (whose name and rank I don't recall) then screamed an instruction for us not to break step or break rank and march in a straight line and not be like the puffs from the other countries (or words to that effect) and so on we marched.

Horse shit flew everywhere. It went up our uniforms, ruining the perfect whiteness of the webbing and sploshed onto the onlookers, who squealed and shouted, whilst trying to back off from the mad British matelot's ploughing on through the shit regardless.

A sort of metaphor for Great Britain in some ways...

HMS Antrim was a County Class Destroyer, with a variety of armament systems. The primary one being Seaslug, an anti-aircraft guided missile system. It also possessed a twin-barrelled MkVI 4.5 inch (114mm) gun turret, two x quad mounted Seacat missile launchers, a pair of 20mm

Oerlikon machine guns and many mounts for 7.62mm GPMG's (General Purpose Machine Guns)

The Seaslug had a twin launcher and was located on the back end, with the missile armoury, loading bays and mechanical / electrical controls stretching almost the length of the ship, with all the other gubbins of messdecks, operations room etc, wrapped around it. Each missile weighed about two tons.

We had a Seaslug test firing on the maritime range off Aberporth, when all the electrical / mechanical systems, communications protocols are fully tested in a much slowed down series of actions over the course of many hours. During that time, no personnel were allowed on the upper decks. Seaslug was a solid fuel propellant missile and there were lots of flames involved in the launch. In order to ensure that no stupid matelot's would become barbecued, hatch sentry's were appointed. Essentially a bloke stood (or sat) by fully clipped hatch, responsible for ensuring no-one opened it.

There I am, sat in the gloom of the passageway, next to a hatch that led onto the flight deck, right down the arse end of the ship. Complete with the health and safety issued ear defenders (over the ear mufflers attached to a strap that sat on the top of your head. I also had a torch (it was dark) and my current paperback book to read.

I had been told that the test firing would likely be during my watch, or the one after me and to make sure I wore my ear defenders. I would know there would be a firing as the missile makes a right racket as it trundles along into the launcher. As it was very hot down there and I was sweating like a whore, I had the ear defenders clipped over my shoulder as I figured I would have time to put them on before the missile was launched, knowing to recognise the trundling sound as a warning.

I have always liked reading and was devouring the pages by torchlight when I heard this massive rumbling sound that went on for a minute or so and sensibly placed the ear defenders in the position they were intended and the rumbling sounds were muffled greatly. Then there was an enormous BOOM sound.

I thought that wasn't too bad and took off the ear defenders. Not realising that the boom had been caused when the armoured doors of the magazine were closed behind the missile sat in the launcher.

It is not possible to describe the noise that was made when the Seaslug was fired. I can only say it was a sort of an immense WHOOSH thing but I was concentrating on slapping my hands over my ears to stop the pain and ringing noise running through my brain and eyes.

The noise was exceedingly loud and sudden. It was fucking awful and temporarily deafened me. It seemed to be days before the pain and tinnitus died down but I couldn't tell a soul what had happened for pure embarrassment.

Reading books was my main occupation at sea in any spare time, in between physical training (a jog round the upper deck – 7 laps made a mile) as I was trying to get into the ships football team, the occasional movie shown late in the dining hall and playing cards.

There were really only two games played in 2E mess (Two Deck, compartment E – fifth from the front, the pointy bit) where we lived. Nominations and three card brag. We bet money on both.

Gambling of course was illegal in the Navy and we were playing for money. Our trick was to operate with a bank. This consisted of a drawer in someone's locker in the mess square. We owned a bag of leather washers picked up when Dusty (the stores branch people) were clearly having an off day and left them loafing about. The washers were our chips and you bought them from the banker, who held all the money.

That way, whenever anyone of authority and that is a wide collection of individuals, who could enter the mess (after knocking on the "door") would only see us playing for tokens. If they knew there was a bank and these were chips they never said. To all intents and appearances, it was an innocent activity. Yeh.

Innocent enough until we caught Carl Rawson cheating at 3-card brag and had to have words with him. His favourite trick was to go "blind" thereby forcing all the other players to bet double his stake or fold. He was remarkably lucky at it.

However, in his case, there was no luck. He liked to wear a hat, not a service issue but a small trilby-type thing and wore it low down over his eyes and would regularly lounge back into the bench seating in the mess and get his eye-level down at the table and could obviously see a lot of the cards being dealt. His normally laid back and lounging persona was masking his cheating and it took a while before we noticed it and it got to the stage that no-one would have him at their card table until he changed his ways.

I had played 3-card brag since I was at school playing for pennies and used a very simple approach. Play carefully until I have about twice the stake I started with. Pocket my original stake and then bet rashly and aggressively as I figured by then, I was playing with someone else's money. I didn't consider it mine until we ended for the evening and cashed out with the banker.

The biggest pot I ever won was £119. A funny number but I have never forgotten it. Given we were being paid about £20 a week, it was pretty bountiful.

Living, working, eating, whingeing and socialising with the same group of people who inhabit a mess (a steel compartment) of limited size puts a lot of pressure on all the relationships, of all the people within it. In our case, we had 39 lads in a space measuring about 30' by 30' made up of a mess square with 15 bunks in it and two annexes with 12 bunks in each.

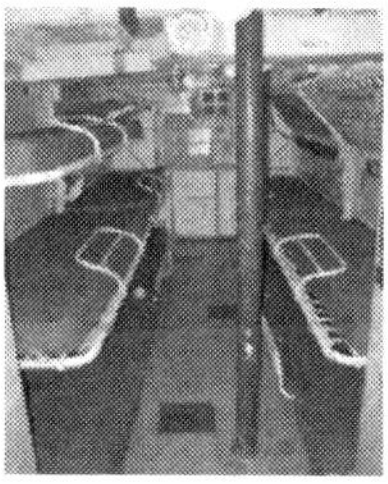

Not everyone in the mess is everyone's friend. We may be messmates but sometimes the tensions and frictions would emanate into squabbles and fisticuffs. As a rule, we all tried hard to maintain composure, even under a barrage of verbal abuse in the guise of funnies, or wind ups or just old-fashioned piss taking. Snowflakes didn't last long in that environment.

It wasn't possible to do anything without someone else knowing what you were doing. Having a fag, going for a dump and having a wank.

It becomes a base existence of humour by its lowest denominator and do something, anything outside of what may be considered normal behaviour. Bear in mind the bar had already been set at very low, almost underground level, the audience would be merciless in its assault on you.

I'm off to curl one down would be a matter of fact statement, as would the greeting on return, had a good shit? Would be a common exchange, similar to, had a good wank?

Queuing up for the heads (toilets) or bathroom (sinks and showers). The forward bathroom had to cater for three messes on the Antrim, 2E with 39 radio operators and other branches dotted around, 3D where 45 or so radar plotters and other miscellaneous sailors would reside and 3E where about 90 gunners and other operational sailors lived below us.

Serving that mass of men was a single piss stone (steel) that could take 5 matelots side by side and 8 traps. Across the flat were the 8 showers and 12 sinks. For circa 150 matelots.

You just got used to queuing, in an orderly fashion. Matching attire of flip flops and towel round your waist carrying your "dhoby bag" of razor, brush, soap (in a box), toothbrush and paste. Nose to tail with a constant loud commentary coming from the queue behind. Hurry up you knob. You've missed a bit and left whiskers on your chin. Hey you crabbie cunt, rinse the bowl off properly before you move on.

Stood in the showers was a lottery of verbal and physical abuse. Wet towels flicked out to cause bruises and cuts were a constant challenge. Squirting shampoo onto the head of someone desperately trying to rinse off the suds until realising that it was due to the torrent of additional shampers being deployed by others. Only for so long as no-one ever wanted to run out of stuff to get you clean and reducing the smelliness of yourself. At sea, personal resources were hard to get hold of.

The smell of a ship is a combination of sweat, oil and grease. It never goes away because the ship never stops working (unless it goes into dock for a refit). The engines turn over, the pipes are constantly pumping and people are cleaning, painting or carrying out training exercises. It just never seems to end.

So daily showering and shaving becomes the norm. Woe betide any "crabs" in the mess. People who didn't wash or shower enough would hum, literally. You could smell them from across the mess and rarely lasted long.

Mess mates would challenge them constantly to go get a shower and if they didn't, action would be taken to throw them into the shower, often fully dressed and have a variety of industrial cleaning products poured over them, in an effort to get them to see the error of their ways.

When I first got aboard the Antrim, we didn't have a fridge. Not too much of a problem in the winter as our beer was stowed in a lockable cleaning cupboard adjacent to the ships side. It was generally cold, clammy and sometimes had condensation on the inside of the locker.

Since the Navy stopped the "Tot" (the daily issue of Rum that went back to the 17th century) on 31st July 1970, quite often referred to as "Black Tot Day" beer had been issued on the basis of three cans per man (aged 18 or over) per day. The can size was about 300ml. Not enough to get you drunk of course but at sea was an element of your right to drink.

Not everyone wanted their beer at sea, for all sorts of reasons. More so in times of big naval exercises when the entire ship went into Defence Watches for a period of time. The majority of roles on a warship conform to a four-watch system. First and Second Port, First and Second Starboard.

Those watches were delivered as your professional delivery. In our case as radio operators manning the Main Communication Office (MCO) and Bridge, with other duties in the Communications Control Room, (CCR) Ultra High Frequency Room (UHF) and the flagdeck. Plus putting up the Union Jack and Royal Ensign at Dawn and Dusk.

In addition to the watches, there would be working parties to maintain the "part of ship" your department was responsible for. Paint what didn't move and grease or polish everything else, plus lots of sweeping up, dusting down and mopping out.

The watch and work rota was:

Comms Watch	**Times**	**Hours worked**	**Part of ship**	**Hours worked**	**Total hours worked**
Forenoon & First	0800-1200 and 2000-2359	8	1300-1600	3	11
Afternoon & Middle	1200-1600 and 0001-0400	8	0800-1130	3.5	11.5
First Dog & Morning	(1600-1800 and 0400-0800	6	0800-1200	4	10
Last Dog and all night in	1800-2000	2	0900-1200 and 1300-1600	6	8

The four-day roster at sea had us working 40 hours every 4 days, with no rest days. Duties were relaxed a little once we got alongside but sea time was demanding and averaged about 80 hours a week, more when we had to replenish at sea.

So it wasn't good if you picked up any punishment like number nine (just known as "NINES") with up to 5 hours additional work in the day, scrubbing pans in the galley (subject to which watch you may be on that particular day)

Late into the summer in 1976, we were sailing from Pompey to the much warmer climes of the middle east, via the Med, the Suez and numerous exercises planned with NATO and CENTRO forces. Visits to places like Alexandria in Egypt, The Seychelles, Karachi in Pakistan, Bandar Abbas in Iran and a few others.

Not having a fridge or a fan in 2E mess was going to be a problem. "Rocky" Semple a complete character of a lad and I were despatched to stores to pick up a fridge. We set off in the ships land rover and held a chitty from our chief storeman.

We got to the main store in the dockyard. "It's one for one" stated the storeman (nicknamed Dusty's). "Well we haven't got one and is why we are here" says Rocky. "I have a chitty".

"Chitty doesn't mean a thing" said the bored Dusty, "you need to bring your old one in and swap it, one for one"

"Right" says Rocky. Who grabs me and drags me out to the jeep. He proceeds to drive round the back of the stores and we sit in the jeep smoking fags for a while.

Then the back of stores open and someone's old fridge gets dropped into the dumper. "There it is" announces Rocky, "our old fridge"

We wait a while for other shit to get dumped and the back doors to the store are secured. Then we climb in, drag out the battered fridge and stow it in the back of the Land Rover.

Another fag and then we drive round the front, into the store and Rocky says to a new desk jockey, “Hey up Dusty, we need a new fridge and we’ve got a chitty”

“No good without the old one, we only swap one for one”

“Sure thing” says Rocky “Moz, go get the old fridge out of the jeep”

So, I trot out, grab the fridge and drag it in. “Great” says the storeman, who stamps Rocky’s chitty, disappears and returns with a new LEC fridge. Hey! We had a new fridge for the mess to keep the beer cold on our travels. All we needed then was a fan.

We finally got a fan fitted in 2E Mess, on the day we sailed from Pompey. The CEM/Chippy fitting it warned the boys in the mess square that unlike all the hurricane fans fitted in all the other messes, ours didn’t have a guard on it and we had to watch out for chopped fingers. Matelots don’t particularly like chopped off fingers so we all gave it a wide berth and it was the cleanest part of the locker mountain. No berets, t-shirts or dhoby rags were left anywhere near it.

So, the deployment to warmer climes got underway with a large combined naval exercise off the Iberian coast “Ocean Safari” and it was, as we seemed to wander all over the place. We were part of blue force escorting a convoy from the Atlantic into and across the Mediterranean Sea under continual attack from orange forces. We were on Defence watches for several weeks, it could have been four or five, I am not sure, which turns everyone into robots. On watch, off watch, eat, sleep and shit. Replenish At Sea (RAS) an activity that draws every able person on the ship to take part (regardless what watch you may have been on). Part of shop maintenance was minimised as we continue to “fight” and respond to action stations etc.

The Antrim was part of the First Flotilla though the “Flag” Vice Admiral Morton and his staff were embarked on HMS Devonshire and accompanied by a number of frigates, submarines and fleet auxiliary vessels carrying all the food, water and fuel that the flotilla would need for the forthcoming exercises.

Refuelling, re-arming and bringing onboard additional potable water and food (plus beer) whilst at sea was a spectacular exercise that tested the ship's capabilities to the full. In exercise, a screen of the flotillas active ships and submarines, acting as the first line of defence would be spread around and each surface warship which would come alongside the auxiliary vessels. Sometimes two warships (one either side) would form up and I have seen photographs of three warships between two fleet auxiliary's steering the same course in a tight formation.

It tests seamanship skills to keep the ships in the correct position at all times during the RAS and teamwork. Once a line or lines have been fired across between the ships and the necessary fuelling pipes or cables with jacks and stays have been put into place for the solid stores, the RAS can begin. There is a lot of manual labour as the crates are hauled over from the stores ship to the deck of the warship, where the pallets are broken down and matelot's handball the goods from the deck, to the secure store rooms below.

It is also a test of the ingenuity of Jack, to try and steal as much contraband as possible for the mess without getting caught. A great challenge for each RAS as Dusty and the NAAFI guys onboard knew exactly what we would do and try their utmost to foil it.

At sea, the lack of access to goodies creates a level of demand that I have only seen demonstrated in prisons (other than the need to escape, create weapons or try and kill each other) cigarettes and beer are standard fare. Three cans of beer a day and eight hundred fags a month could be bought without problem. Everything else assumed positions of luxury items and held values of such throughout the ship.

So Dusty knows that Jack is going to try and steal as much as they can and position themselves at strategic points around the ship to keep an eye on the human chains handballing the goodies. NAAFI personnel take up position on the deck (to count them in) and by the secure storage for beers (junior rates) and the hard alcohol (senior rates and officers) and we in turn would deploy decoy's to look suspicious when the beer crates were being chucked about but were actually after things like tins of fruit salad, ham and other canned goods that could be stowed away quickly and kept for some time before they needed to be consumed, in the silent hours of middle and morning watches.... We were almost always successful.

The Devonshire had a bad accident when a boiler blew up killing and maiming a few stokers. The Devonshire returned to UK for repairs and to manage the funerals for the sadly deceased and medical support for the injured.

This resulted in the Admiral Flag Officer First Flotilla (FOF1) being transferred over to The Antrim and brought with it all the flag duties. i.e. in charge of all manoeuvres and all communications. The Almirante Gago Coutinho (a Portuguese frigate of dubious capability) at the end of the exercise requested every single signal sent by FOF1 over the course of the four to five week exercise. The plonkers.

All the time, the fan is swinging from side to side, blowing warm and less-warm air about the mess square. Not sure it cooled us down at all but we respected its efforts and stayed well clear of the vicious looking blades. At least we had cold beer from a fridge (thank you Rocky and Moz).

Clear of the exercise, we went down the Suez and not sure if it was the SMP (Short Maintenance Period) first in the Seychelles or after we exercised with the Pakistan and Indian Navies. My first experience of a "SUB DOWN" when a Pakistani submarine failed to make its appointed communications calls. We had every radio operator dangling off every available radio frequency for days in case they managed to get a distress call out. However, it turned out to be a complete communications system failure on the submarine, which was happily sailing home without telling anyone. Cheers.

One of our trips was to Bandar Abbas following a series of exercises with the Iranian fleet (when we were still friends) and whilst Iran even then, was under various levels of martial law, we were allowed ashore to attend specific events. A wonderful indoor BBQ I can recall and the sports club at Lockheed, which is where Bilbo and the fan reached acclaim.

Bilbo (Steve Bielby) a chunky bunting from Hull, had gone to the sports club in the second wave (afternoon piss-up) and was not aware of the broken beer glasses and bottles that had ended up in the swimming pool from the earlier piss-up. However, after completing his ritual "Zulu Warrior" performance, he was showered in beer from those cheering him on. Covered in the sticky substance, Bilbo decided to clean himself off in the pool.

Always the attention grabber, he climbed the diving board and swallow dived in the pool, skirting the bottom of the pool, where one of the large pieces of glass stuck in his pectoral muscle and screwed a little bit towards his sternum. He surfaced in a red mist and bits of flapping tit. Cue great first aid response as people jumped into the pool and grabbed his chest to hold the wound together. Then off he went to the first aid post and on to the Antrim. Not sure who sewed him up.

Back on board the wound got longer and deeper with every retelling of the story until the gash went from his throat to his groin and he must be dead for sure. Lights out and a small crowd of us are still in the mess square seeing off some tins when Bilbo's standard greeting call echoed down the passageway "Oh Eh?" multiple times and getting louder as he neared 2E Mess. "Fucking hell, he's here and alive!" Bilbo, wearing only a pair of skidders, had made his way "home" from the Antrim sick bay where he had been lain for the night, complete with a taped-up dressing on his chest.

In response to queries about his general health Bilbo rips off the dressing to show everyone his stitches and says "Look, if you squeeze it, this colourless liquid seeps out and then it bleeds" everyone sort of leans back as much as possible from him to avoid getting splashed in it when Bilbo suddenly shouts out and jumps up "That fucking fan is freezing and its pissing me off" and does no more than to clamber up the bunks and shove his hand straight into the spinning blades!!

We all expected to see more blood and pieces of digit slinging about the place but all that happened was a "blub, blub, blub" sound as the rubber blades slowly came to a stand, at which point we all burst out laughing. As much for the lack of damage to Bilbo but at the wind up put in place by the CEM/Chippy many weeks before and not being there to see the result of his handiwork. Funny guy.

After successfully completing a number of exercises, with NATO and CENTRO partners, we were in need of an Assisted Maintenance Period, more than just re-arming, fuelling up, taking on water and large amounts of victuals, some of the key systems needed their regular overhaul so they get switched off and took apart, cleaned, greased, essential components replaced and rebuilt. An opportunity to paint the superstructure following the relentless war against salt erosion and other good stuff like that. During the naval exercises and in particular having FOF1 onboard, generated a lot of communications traffic, between the fleet and back to UK.

Normally the confidential waste is shredded daily but it was difficult to keep up with the volume, so some of it gets bagged (paper gash sacks) and stowed in the confidential waste locker. A tiny compartment underneath one of the radar assemblies. Requiring the radar to be turned off (no-one wants their nuts frying in a RadHaz incident) and sets of keys to be drawn from the wheelhouse. This was also our "secret beer stowage"

(We drew out the allotted amount of 3 x cans of beer per over-18, regardless of whether they were drunk – very little during an exercise, paying for the extra through "mess funds" the bank but we had too much for the fridge and the cleaning gear locker and so needed somewhere secure to stow it.

Each night the RO's would clean up for Officers Rounds and take extra gash sacks of beer, along with the bona fide confidential waste, up the mast). We had a 2-day mammoth piss up in Karachi for anyone lucky enough to be invited to the 2E Mess party and can remember it…. That is where the beer came from. Our secure beer stowage up the mast.

Part way through the exercise, the shredder bust. “Unrepairable” was the REM diagnosis. Dusty would no doubt not swap it out until we got back alongside, somewhere, with a chitty of course… so more and more bags were stowed.

We had already had problems shredding carbon paper (everything was duplicate or triplicate in those analogue days) and so the bags had “CARBON” china graphed onto their sides to warn it couldn’t be shredded and had to be burnt.

As part of the many communications before arriving in port, we requested access to an incinerator to dispose of the hundreds and hundreds of bags of confidential waste.

When we finally got alongside in Mahe, we got the news that incinerators didn’t exist in the Seychelles.

Not to be undone, a little initiative was demonstrated (by person or persons unknown) to borrow a 50-gallon oil drum shoreside and burn the confidential waste ourselves….

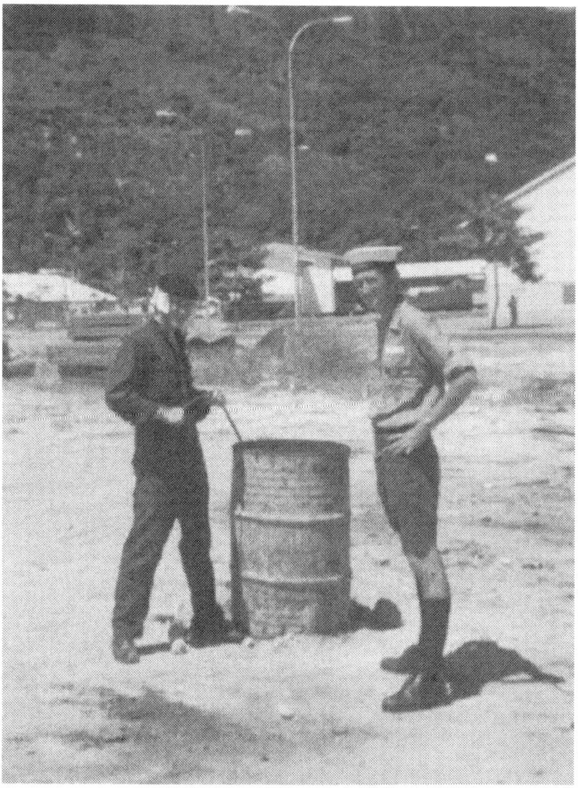

Typical Royal Navy, a procedure for burning waste in an oil drum was written up, which went something like:

1. Put a small amount of paper (screwed up) in the bottom of the oil drum.
2. Light it with a taper.
3. Slowly feed the contents of the gash sack into the oil drum, in single sheets, to ensure that they all burn
4. Use the large steel pinch bar to gently stoke the embers and wait until it has burnt out before commencing the process again.

All very sound words no doubt and sounding very sensible, when typed up in the quiet of the MCO.

However, out on the jetty it was chuffing hot. High 30's, unrelenting sun and stood close to the oil drum was equally unpleasant.

Amended (and unwritten) procedure developed inside the first 48 hours...

1. Get 3 more drums.
2. Empty half a gash sack into each oil drum.
3. Drop lit clutch of confidential papers into the drum.
4. Hold half full gash sack over and into the oil drum and draw back upwards a couple of times to get plenty of air around the ignited papers.
5. Pull bag away sharply, avoid whoosh of flames that head skywards.
6. Put bag on mound of bags under tarpaulin covered pallets (shade).
7. Get all 4 drums alight the same way and retire to the shade for limers and a ciggie or a sneaky bronzie.
8. Open more bags and pour onto already burning paper and repeat actions from 4. Onwards.

This way, more bags are burned and less time is spent stood up getting hot and bothered, sweaty and sunburnt.

Ahead of this of course, we came alongside and the first half of the ships company are given 48 hours “station leave” and I was part of that initial surge ashore coming off a morning watch as we berthed. Following a hearty breakfast, we ran ashore complete with towels and speedo’s, then boarded the lorries (buses) with plank seats in the back and bounced over the island to the wonderful Beau Vallon Bay. An idyllic place complete with a beach shack bar, 2E Mess made a base camp at the bar and proceeded to down beers and cocktails.

A few foray’s into the water, a stroll up the beach with a machete to chop down some coconuts (an illegal act by all accounts but no-one stopped us) and those who had prepared well, lay down to top up the tans as the toll of Defence Watches caught up with us all. The watch spread out and hit the Z’s.

This had been the longest time I done watch about, and during the down time all I did was hit my pit and count the Z’s – sprog that I was. Everyone else spent half an hour or so, sometimes longer on the upper scupper getting a basic tan. I couldn’t see the benefit and just needed sleep. Having a ginger minge, fair hair and freckles, I could never be described as a sun-lover….

This of course came back to haunt me that day at Beau Vallon Beach. Nicknamed the White Shadow on the day (as can be seen in the photographic evidence).

I didn't attempt to catch the rays like everyone else. I nodded in the shade but went off with Bilbo and a couple of others to cut down and eat coconuts. Cadge a lift in a boat and went snorkelling off the coral reefs before heading back to RV at the beach bar.

Late afternoon now. We had snacked on burgers and stuff from the bar, whilst supping a lot. I had gone from being the White Shadow to a well singed tomato, having rapidly progressed through fried prawn. However, whilst my sunburn was bad, it was by nowhere near the worst.

We had done a buddy check and noticed that Eddy (Mark Eddiford) had disappeared. No-one had seen Eddy since about lunchtime. He was found fast asleep on the other side of a breakwater, having lain on his back the entire time. His back was clear but his face, chest and legs were a mess. Similar to Moz but much, much worse.

Under advice from more experienced colleagues, Moz and Eddy thought it best to head back to the ship whilst the rest of the watch stayed on the beach and in fact spent most of that first 24 hours either swimming, sleeping or drinking on the beach.

Eddy and Moz got back to the ship and it was agreed with messmates, not to report into the sick bay as we would both be on a ticket for self-inflicted injuries. Some calamine lotion was cadged and most of it was poured onto the now sizzling Eddy. I think we could have fried eggs on his chest, he was that hot. He is still scarred by it today I believe....

Moz's sunburn scabbed over whilst Eddy's sort of formulated over the next 24 hours. Then we had to pick up duties again. We all pitched in and covered Eddy's watches on the 3rd day, no matter what they were. It was a while before he got back on his feet properly.

Meanwhile, the confidential waste burning continued and I, as sprog of our watch, was a nominated "burner" and did a number of duties out there. We burned 24/7 for several days and it was on one of the dog watches, my mess mates were off out on the piss whilst I was stoking and pouring bags of confidential waste into the oil drums. They were taking the piss out of me. In the gloom, I failed to notice "CARBON" scrawled on the brown paper gash sack and just followed our amended routine.

I opened the bag and doshed the contents onto the still burning previous load. Whilst shouting abuse back to the departing matelots. Someone noticed the flame burst up into the bag as I was looking over my shoulder back at them. They shouted something, I told them to fuck off and yanked the bag out. Cue massive column of flame shooting out of the oil drum and me with arms outstretched upwards. Boom!

It burnt off my eyebrows, eyelashes and all the hair exposed, a v-shape on my chest and everything else on my short-sleeved arms...... my mates came back and we hastily concocted a story around the amended procedure and helped me to sick bay. The medic gave me attention but could not understand why there was burnt skin on my chest, shoulders, arms and legs. I had to say I didn't understand either but managed to get my beach burn hidden by the incineration event and wangle 2 days light duties! Bonus.

We continued to burn confidential waste on the jetty in Mahe, The Seychelles, running 24/7. On a watch changeover Rocky asks me to help him move an 8 x 4 sheet of hardboard next to the shaded caboose and cover it in palm fronds and other debris. Then disappeared back to the ship for a break. He returned to relieve me later on and said, let's see what we caught. All the time in the dark you could hear the cockroaches scuttling about and occasionally see their shadows from the burning oil drums but they stayed well away from the fires.

We each grabbed a corner and folded the sheet into a bend and the leaves started writhing with all the cockies in there. Rocky shoves his end over a burning oil drum then helps me to heave my end up, pouring hundreds of cockroaches into the flames. After only a moment or two, they started popping like small fireworks or popcorn in a pan. Hilarious. We repeated it several times over the following watches.

As gorgeous as the Seychelles was, I have never seen so many big cockroaches in all my life. They were massive.

We were in Mahe for 10 days, carrying out repairs, maintenance and painting. The last couple of days we had to anchor off as a large stores ship needed to get alongside. The Seychelles like lots of islands around the world are nowhere near self-sufficient anymore. Anchoring off meant we had to utilise the dreaded boat routine, which created a much greater barrier to getting bladdered. You had to report in at the jetty (seen by officah's and senior rates), transfer by ships boat to the mother vessel (often accompanied by a senior rate), where there was another chance to be inspected by the Officah of the Day and the Quarter Master. Depending on who it was, you either had an easy ride or you didn't. Never seemed to be much in between. This was usually a deterrent to "bad behaviour" but not always…. This one was tropical rig, another deterrent to travelling, so we had full white No.1's on, which of course have their drawbacks as well as opportunities….

The last night we had a weather warning, that we were going to head into a tropical thunderstorm the day of departure, plus despite the cheap beer in Mahe, a lot of the boys had run out of beer funds. Big Dave Pristaw said "C'mon Moz, lets get ashore on the last night" but I told him I had run out of beer chitties and he agreed and said that so had he but we would send the cap round. Confused, I didn't understand. So Big Dave shouts out through the Mess, is anyone coming ashore with me and Moz. Lots of negative replies, so he says, "Right then, give us all your shrapnel so me and Moz can get ashore for a last couple of beers. Everyone complies. Rupee's off all denominations end up in the beret. A massive pile of coins. Lots of funny remarks about how we were going to impress the bar staff counting out ickies for beers. Ha ha. Who had the last laugh?

As soon as we got ashore Big Dave headed straight to a shop and asked the person at the counter if they needed change. Of course they do, all shops do. Big Dave comes out smiling wafting a wad of notes like a second-hand car dealer and shouts "On we go!"

We had a cracking night, supped a lot of beers and cocktails courtesy of our benevolent mess-mates. We were in a club dancing with some Scandinavian girls who didn't speak English but clearly attracted to the white suited dancers (Big Dave and Moz) glowing in the ultra violet lights quite popular in 70's discos (though not for those with dandruff of course). Not sure their boyfriends could speak English either but gave me and Dave the evil eye (international communication) as we danced with their birds. Great fun. We even had enough notes left at the end of the night to trade in with the Supply Officer the next day when his little bank was open. Bonus!

We had to be careful though, with being on boat routine. We did aim to get the second last liberty boat, that way, our plan had a get out, the last liberty boat! Good plan as we were accosted by the lovely ladies of the night staffing the big piles of plastic drainage pipes along the dockyard road, which evidently provided shelter and privacy for horizontal dancing....... All available for just a handful of klebbies.....

It is hard keeping track of currency, the rates etc. when you are visiting lots of different places around the world. Matelots have a simple arrangement. All coins are known as "Ickies" and all notes are known as "Klebbies". All you need to know about being on foreign land is how many ickies and klebbies there are to a quid. Once you know that, everything is easy peasy.

Anyway, as the second last liberty boat returned to the mother ship, we sat on the jetty with a number of other drunken souls watching the cockroaches scuttle about. A particular monster one caught Dave's eye and he threw his cap over it. I guess we expected the result to be Dave walking over, picking up the cap and crushing the cockie under his boot. Not so. His cap started shuffling across the jetty, powered by the "super-cockie" scuttling underneath. Dave commented on its strength and motoring abilities. Then picked up his cap and stood on it. For almost a complete second Big Dave was suspended in the air, held up only by the "super cockie". Which then squelched as Big Dave came down to earth.

We all laughed a lot. And looked around to see if we could find any more but none as big or as strong as that bugger.

Then the last liberty boat came alongside the jetty wall. Not one of our ship's boats but a local big flat bellied thing with plenty of space for all the late departures. This was after all, the last one. It was low tide and we had to clamber down a near vertical ladder to it. Then we sat and waited for the allotted departure time. Suddenly there was a call over the radio, for the boat to make way for the skipper's Hunter. He had been ashore on a function and had a small entourage with him. The last liberty boat was instructed to stand off for a few minutes so the Hunter could pick up the official party, then it could haul back alongside for the last sailors.

Ropes loosened and the big wooden boat slowly heaved off the jetty when in the darkness, 3 matelots appeared. One slung between the shoulders of his two oppo's clearly making sure he got back onboard. Next thing one shouts "Don't go without Bungy!" and the two outriders do no more than sling "Bungy" about ten feet out into the air, clearly aiming for the boat but missing it by about 3 feet. We all looked up in surprise as "Bungy" flew over our heads and into the sea, where he began to sink.

The two outriders then jumped and clattered in amongst us, laughing like hell and then said "Where's Bungy?" Luckily, one of the local lads on the boat had a barge pole and hook, which he used to hook the drowning Bungy's uniform and pull him onto the boat. Initial shock, lots of laughter and even more so after the royal party was picked up and we went back alongside to await the last dregs of the run ashore. Epic night.

After exercising with the Indian and Pakistani navles, who both had to operate independently from each other since the war only a few years ago, had left a lot of tension in the area, we headed to the Pakistan naval port in Karachi.

We got to Karachi after the exercise,(this is the one where the Pakistani submarine failed to communicate and all the RO's dangled off every available frequency for a few days. Turned out it had had a comms failure so just sailed home without being able to tell anyone it was safe.

It was an interesting run ashore. We went Onyx hunting and my particular bag of rabbits included 6 x goblets and an ashtray, bartered down from something extortionate, to something I thought I could afford. No opportunity for a beer that we found, so we retired back to the ship and had our mess 2-day piss up with oodles of beer, bit of singing, bit of dancing and a lot of laughs.

We had lots of visitors over the 2-days, lads from other messes, the padre (always liked a drink) and a number of officers joined us. The routine was always the same in those days. A guest was anyone invited by any member of the mess, was not allowed to buy any beer and someone in the mess always made sure the visitor had at least three cans on arrival and a non-stop service of free beer until they left, or were thrown out.

The communications department broken shredder once again demanded the use of an incinerator after we got alongside in the Pakistan naval base. Arrangements were made to turn off the radar, get the keys from the wheelhouse and head up to the oven in the mast to collect the stowed bags of confidential waste. At the same time, relieving a large number of gash sacks full of cans of CSB and Heineken Export, which were diverted down to 2E Mess.

To get into the confidential waste store, one had to climb up a vertical ladder and push a hatch up to its retaining spring lock. A challenge in the heat of a ship sat in the sun all day. Much more of a challenge at sea, when the height of the mast amplified the roll creating risks of trapped limbs in the hatch and requiring superhuman strength to push the hatch up against the gravity of the rocking and rolling, or alternatively superhumanly flying up through the hatch as the ship pitched down.

Once the hatch was up, the devilishly low deckhead restricted how you hauled your body up and into this tiny space (not one for the claustrophobics) and then lay on your back, you inched your way to the other side of the compartment, to lift yet another hatch that led up to the radar base and where all the confidential waste was stowed. In that sun, it was "redders" and sweat ran down everything. We formed a chain and chucked the waste down (whilst carefully lowering the precious, if by now very warm, bags of beer). Until we emptied the store.

Waiting for us on the jetty was a flat-bed truck, with short hinged side panels. We loaded up several hundred bags of waste. 2 matelots could sit in the cab with the driver. No air conditioning, just big windows wound right down. The rest of us stood on the flat bed, right behind the cam and hanging onto its roof and we set off through and out of the dockyard and drove a few miles down the road.

At first, the traffic held us up and it was fairly scenic journey, then I saw my first dead bodies in Karachi. Mostly just curled up on the side of the road, with people walking past and stepping over them. I couldn't understand the lack of humanity towards them…… and still don't to be honest.

The traffic cleared and the lorry speeded up. The road surface was shit and when we hit the first pothole about a dozen bags leapt up into the air and the rush of wind caused by the speeding up, distributed them across the street behind us. Cue several bangs on the cab roof to get the attention of the driver and get him to pull over. Then we all had to jog up the dusty street and retrieve the bags before any of them were snaffled. Loss of confidential waste would have been a trip over the wall at the very least. We did get them all back thankfully. The Pakistani navy driver shouted a lot at the people that started to gather and so they stood off and watched a load of red-faced matelots gather in the gash sacks and reload the lorry.

Don't remember the Killick RO who led us that day but he initiated a security procedure that involved all the RO's present to lie on the bags, on the flatbed, alarmingly higher than the short hinged sides as we continued our journey to the incinerator. Solved the security scare for sure but imported a serious health and safety risk that I am sure would not be tolerated in today's mob…. To be fair, the driver didn't go as fast has he had previously, so at least someone thought about those of us acting as dead-weights on the back….

The incinerator turned out to be a stand-alone unit, outside in what appeared to be a large joiner's yard. We couldn't fit all the bags in the incinerator in one go and took at least a couple of sittings. Fill the incinerator. Ignite it. Watch the fire through a glass panel. Wait for the flames to die down. Re-fill and wait. We got through a lot of fags between us for sure.

It was hot and we tried to find what shade we could. We were also "harry" driers as no-one had thought to bring any victuals with us and certainly nothing to drink. Limers would have gone down a treat.... Asking around one of the boys was directed to a shiny copper sink, with a shiny stainless steel tap in it. Part of another stand-alone construction. There was a rush to get to the sink and drink from the tap.

I just looked up and saw this manky looking tank on top of the construction, which in effect, was a miniature water tower. All I could think of was stagnant water and cockroaches...... so didn't avail myself of the drink and went thirsty until we got back to the ship. Not sure if anyone was really, really ill but a couple of the boys had the trots for a while.

In the downtime from major exercises we patrolled the Straights of Hormuz, Gulf of Aden and pottered around the Red Sea, with the ship carrying out its daily challenge of fighting the rust and practising fighting fires and preventing the ship from sinking. It was also time for "Captains Rounds" a quarterly event that stretched everyone.

We had to affect a deep clean of all the messes, including storage areas, the passageways and all work-spaces. It was clearly intended to make sure the ship remained as healthy an environment as possible and a lot of attention was paid to lockers, bunks, bedding and clothes storage areas. 2E Mess had one communal wardrobe. Except it wasn't a wardrobe, it was a steel locker about ten feet long and 3 feet deep that had to house all the civilian clothes belonging to 39 men, our navy overcoats and it was protected by a flimsy curtain.

I have seen less space taken up by one woman's clothing, let along 39 men. What could be hung up was. What couldn't be hung up was stowed in holdalls, suitcases and boxes, all piled up and squeezed in to take advantage of every cubic inch of space. It wasn't a pretty sight. Bags were usually packed with our civvy go-ashore-stuff the night before we sailed from anywhere and there was a general lack of care at that particular moment when you are readying for sea.

Stuff was dragged out a few days before we landed anywhere and exposed to the Chinese Laundry down at the back of the ship (the blunt end), to create a going ashore outfit.

Not a well-known fact in civvy street but warships of a certain size, were permitted to carry (under a Hong Kong based contract) a set number of Chinese Laundrymen. The Antrim had a team of 5, along with a Chinese barber and a Chinese tailor, all making small profits for their Hong Kong masters and presumably earning themselves a wage whilst travelling the world.

My first day on board the Antrim, Rocky showed me around (would be classed as an induction these days) and was my buddy in those first few months at sea. He took me to the Laundry because I needed some stuff cleaned and I was introduced to "Number One" who was the boss of the dhoby shack. All the team had numbers, depending on their rank and ours went One to Five. They reckoned we could never pronounce their names and so used numbers.

Number One said that we all looked alike and so gave us numbers. Our number was the last four digits of our official number and that became our laundry number. 7392 in my case. He looked at me for a moment or two and then said "7392" okay. Then waved us away. Very few of them spoke English, which I found interesting and just communicated to us by our laundry numbers and pointing.

I went back a couple of days later for my stuff and before I could speak, Number One looked at me and said "7392" and I, a bit gobsmacked, just nodded and he looking chuffed gave me my little package of clean and ironed stuff.

You had to be careful though, as it wasn't like putting your clothes into a modern machine like today, with settings for cottons, light fabrics or delicates. Everything was boil washed at about 80 degrees. Then steam ironed. Clothes would shrink.

They did a fantastic job on my Number 1 uniform which had clearly been made for a much bigger me (assumption that I would grow) and it was quite baggy. Not after the Chinese dhoby men did their stuff. It was skin-tight and just the job for attracting the ladies to my manly physique....

Taff Powell, a laconic and dry humoured welsh bunting once fell foul of the dhoby men and it was a salutary lesson for all.

The five dhoby men, the tailor and barber would join us for meal-times and I noticed that when they came into the dining hall they didn't automatically sit together but just took the first vacant seat. I also noticed that as they arrived, some guys stood up from their table and filled the gaps on adjacent tables. All in a slow but determined way and filled all eight places at the table. I wondered why they did that until one of the dhoby men sat in front of me and proceeded to eat his meal.

He didn't pick up a knife and fork but used his fingers like a cross between chopsticks and a spoon and shovelled a load of food into his mouth, whilst talking Chinese (or Mandarin, or Cantonese, or whatever) to his mate who was sat on the table behind me, without ever seemingly closing his mouth whilst he chewed, and talked.

The outcome was a steady stream of food bits spitting out of his mouth in different directions, going onto my plate, the plate of the guys either side of me and I got really angry. Rocky, seeing the change in my persona, gripped my arm and said come on let's go and before I could say or do anything, he had shepherded me out and told me it wasn't worth it. Drop our shit into the scullery hatch. Scrape food into a bin and then place, or throw your large steel tray and cutlery onto a pile and shout a greeting like "clean my shit" to your comrades who had been selected for "Scullery Party" for 12-weeks at a time. Who in turn usually resorted with witty repartee shouts of "Fuck Off" in return.

Rocky then ushered me back round and we re-joined the dining hall queue for some fresh food, which by the time we entered the dining hall, was now dhoby-men-less.

Taff Powell knew the routine but somehow failed to be the person joined, nor get up to join others and therefore remained exposed by the vacant seats around and in front of him. On the day in question, Taff was joined by two dhoby men, one beside and one in front of him. They both proceeded to engage in a loud and extensive exchange whilst shovelling food into their mouths with great speed and alacrity, whilst some of it (chewed or unchewed) was spat out in all directions as the ferocity of the exchange continued. Taff did no more than stand up and began a tirade aimed at the dhoby man in front of him, in a vibrant welsh voice.

"Yew dirty bastards, yew fucking dirty cunts, spreading yewer fucking mess all over my fucking dinner yew dirty cunts!"

You could see all the dhoby men looking at him, silently, thinking "4752" as Taff stormed out of the canteen. And so it began.

First of all the dhoby men, when ironing his No.8's work shirt must have hammered the iron down so that all of his buttons were smashed and cracked. He went down to the laundry to remonstrate with Number 1 who apologised and said the tailor would fix, free of charge. Taff took his shirt to the tailor who apologised that he didn't have a full set of buttons but would see what he could do. His number 8 shirt came back with 6 or 7 different sized and different colour of blue and black buttons on it.

Next was one of his sheets, which had been caught by the iron and had a 3-way cut in the material. No to worry said Number 1, the tailor will fix. He did with a square patch sewn on and it looked a bugger.

The final straw was his number 8 pants which somehow had all the stitching removed from the seams on one leg. No problem, said Number 1, they must have boiled off in the washer, you take to the tailor. Who apologised that he didn't have the exact colour of navy blue but did have some royal blue cotton and re-stitched them.

Taff stopped sending his stuff to the laundry and did it all himself after that....

Anyway, getting back to Captains Rounds. Rocky and I had the task of sorting out the coat locker, as our wardrobe was called. His approach was a simple one. Drag everything out and throw it into the passageway and annexe. Then get stuck into washing (with hot soapy water) the sides, the top and the floor of the coat locker.

Then, with me on ironing board duty, we carefully placed everyone's coats, including service burberry raincoats, denim jackets, sheepskin coats and other outer gear onto coat hangers, with my pressing out anything that needed it, making things look "tickety-boo", as we used to say when something neat was being expressed.

The next task was to work through the holdall's to make sure that nothing sinister was lurking inside. This might well include unwashed skidders, beer stained t-shirts and curry covered jumpers, which were bagged into a pillow-case and taken down to the laundry to be washed under my number or Rocky's.

Whilst doing so Rocky shoved a box under my nose and shouted "It's a Chartham Method!" and I being such a naive 18-year old enquired what the hell was a Chartham Method? To which Rocky replied "Its for making your cock bigger!" well you could have knocked me down with a feather. It looked like a big fat test tube, with a tube and a pump attached to it.

Who's is it? I asked enquiringly "What a fucking good question" says Rocky turning the box over to check the name and postal address still attached to it and shouts "It's Lennie's!"

Lennie Barnett was the least liked of all our mess mates, primarily because he used to snitch to the Chief and also whinge a lot. He did have a number of people who did feel sorry for him and try to protect him but Lennie brought on a lot of trouble onto himself.

Rocky knew he was on duty in the MCO and did no more than march down the passageway, past the wheelhouse to the office, opened the door and slid the open box displaying the "Chartham Method" along with a helpful verbal description of its contents and who it belonged to in one fell swoop and it belongs to Lennie.

Everyone looked at the contents of the box as it slid across the MCO floor, then looked over at Lennie who shrieked and kicked out the escape hatch at the far end of the MCO and ran off down the passageway. They all burst out laughing and it was the talk of the ship all day. Though it wasn't funny when Lennie failed to show up for his afternoon work party and despite many broadcasts throughout the ship, he failed to turn up and so we commenced a ship-wide search for him.

Eventually and this was late in the afternoon, he was found up the secure stowage when someone in the wheelhouse wondered why one of the radar mast keys was still signed out, noticed the name L. Barnett and managed to add together with the constant stream of announcements over the ships broadcast. Mastermind.

He was coaxed down by the Chief who called for a clear deck of radio operators. He got us all into the passageway outside the MCO, had the hatches clipped at either end so no-one else could hear and tore a strip of each and every one of us for singling Lennie out in such a terrible way, saying that he was in such a state that he could have taken his own life. A sobering thought.

I decided at that point to scratch the cartoon I had drawn of a giant sized cock sticking up from one of the traps and a caption that read “Lennie you have been in there a long time, are you okay?”

I was part of the team that was responsible for producing the ships newspaper “The Antrim News” throughout my time onboard – MODUK used to send out a 6-page compilation of news headlines, which I found out in a later draft to Northwood, was literally that. One of our egg-crusted finest would highlight sections of several newspapers, which RO’s typed up into the 6-pager that got to every ship, in any part of the world, daily. The old style was to just copy it many times and pin it to various notice boards around the ship and in the messes.

The MCO decided to tart it up a bit. Delete all the comms bumph like signal identity, date, time and page number. Spread out the news with large gaps, then fill the gaps with cartoons, a very rude page 3 that bordered on butchery displays at times, a “blue” crossword and other stuff. Then copy it. No fancy photocopying in the early days, it was “Ormig” fuelled spirit reproducer that usually got the participant covered in a purply-blue dye that got through even a No.8 shirt and stained the skin.

Ormig (in its early days) and Orange Juice provided a surprisingly pleasant alternative to a “screwdriver”, until some bright spark added a formula to the neat spirit rendering it a challenge for even the most ardent alcoholics….

Moz drew the cartoons that went on the front page or were used to highlight a particular story or event. The front page took a life of its own at times. It certainly began in a benign manner but was quickly used to point the finger at funny things that had happened around the ship. I still have some of those original front page cartoons and have included two of them in this post, to emphasise two parts of this ditty.

It got to the point, that matelots from all branches would pull me to one side, when I was about the ship and share a funny event involving a shipmate or mates, which I would try and incorporate into the newspaper. Drawing the cartoons, writing poems and delivering the news would be a positive for me, in what was a time of undulating progression.

Those who remember me, will know that I had a pretty chequered career on the Antrim. Despite becoming proficient in all the comms kit and being invited to lead the watch and help our RS George Bulleyment with "complanning" and stuff there was a darker side to me. Incidents, usually involving alcohol and others when I was stone cold sober got me into a lot of trouble. In 1976 alone I was at the table twice and made two civvie court appearances, all in the space of 7 months. It led to me receiving a break in good conduct, quite a serious thing that hampers advancement in later years evidently.

Drunk and Disorderly in Portsmouth Magistrates Court after exiting Joanna's with 4 glass tankards strapped to my jeans belt under my coat. A very kind sergeant from the Hampshire Constabulary downgraded the criminal charge of theft to" Drunk & Disorderly" as he felt sorry for the sprog 19-year old. I explained that we didn't have any beer glasses in the mess and was being used as a mule to carry them onboard. Didn't quite use those terms but you know what I mean. Haha and no, I couldn't remember who else was with me....

The Sussex Constabulary were less inclined and they did me for Drunk and theft of beer mugs following a night of high jinks and fighting in Brighton with some of my civvy mates (Jack and Bob) from Stockport who had moved to Worthing and ran a Wimpey Bar there. Despite me throwing the glasses away as the police chased me down Worthing high street and them smashing. They bracketed me and I ran into the dead end of the market refuse area. I dived in and dug / swam through the rubbish until I hit a brick wall. Then waited while the 2 coppers pulled all the rubbish away to drag me out and cuff me. Clearly didn't see the funny side of being covered in rotting vegetables. They picked up all the broken glass and charged me. Haha. Another night in a cell.

Our SCO had previously accompanied me to Pompey magistrates and said he had to do the same with the latest charge. I was stood next to him when he said, the court appearance is 10:30. "I will meet you on the jetty at 09:45 and you will need to dress smartly but not in uniform". I just looked at the Brighton Magistrates charted document and thought, this is going to be fun.

I was on the jetty early having a fag when the SCO pulled up in is car. "You are looking all full of yourself Perkins, considering you are about to appear in court, what's so funny?" So I said, "Well Sir, I am not sure how we are going to get to Brighton Magistrates Court in (looking at watch for effect) in a little under 45 minutes. "Brighton!!" roared the SCO, "Brighton, why Brighton?" I replied, "The offence was in Worthing and the charge sheet clearly showed Brighton. I assume you had read it sir?"

He hadn't got enough fuel to drive to Brighton, so I loaned him a fiver. He stopped twice on the way to Brighton to call the court and apologise for our late arrival. I am not sure what he said because he didn't tell me but we got into Brighton and I appeared at 12:30 ish. Fined £25 and politely bollocked by the magistrate. I paid it in one go as I had holiday pay in my wallet and we drove back to Portsmouth along the coast road with the SCO continuing to remonstrate with me about my drunken antics.

Then he asked me what time it was and I said 14:20 and he swore and said "Shit we will miss lunch" and pulled off the coast road into a pub. He bought a pair of beers and I, under my need to be good and demonstrate I am being good, sipped the pint whilst he downed his then shouted "Hurry up Perkins, it's your round next!" Haha. A 4-pint DTS and then he drove me back to the ship continuing to berate me, telling me how good he rated by professional knowledge but that I was a wanker after 16:00. It was hard to argue with him really.

Fighting onboard at sea with a scouse stoker (cannot remember his name, blond curly hair) in the dining hall queue. He pushed me in the back cos the queue wasn't moving fast enough and I did warn him that if he pushed again he would be wearing the plate of food. He did so after his mates egged him on, so he got to wear the food as I plated him in the face with it.

Him and his 2 mates then jumped on me and it was all wild for a while until the chief chef got involved. No dinner for the 4 of us. We both got a week of No.9's. I know we made up in Bristol and the pair of us went on the piss together and got on famously for the rest of the time we served together. I just cannot remember his name.

1977 saw me eliminate civilian court appearances but upped the onboard ante with Drunk and verbally abusing a Master At Arms (The Joss off the Achilles) in which I was almost totally innocent. After bringing a Jock and a Paddy home for the weekend (An Englishmen, Irishman and a Scotsman) no shit.

We had a hectic time in Stockport, a couple of fights, one in which I came off second best and got a broken nose as part of receiving 5 kicks to the head when I went down in a scrap with 2 pongo's and 3 of their civvy mates. So I was already wounded and very, very drunk as we got a train from Stockport, then the last leg, Smoke to Chatham.

The Paddy "Bill" Bailey and I were recounting Monty Python sketches and had the train compartment in stitches. Clearly our loud antics and humour was not to the pleasure of MAA Aylott sat next to me and after whispering several times to me to wind down the volume, he opened his wallet and flashed his ID card, which indeed showed MAA Aylott and it was stamped HMS Achilles.

His identity confirmed I turned to inform Mr Bailey who launched into a tirade that went along the lines of "I can smell pork in here, can anyone else?" as I tried to wave him down, he stood to shout around the compartment "a little piggy wiggy and he is sat just there" at which point Mr Aylott moved away from us.

We arrived in Chatham and unbeknown to us, he got in the taxi queue behind us, jumped the queue as we took off and followed us in. We got onboard, collected station cards and got into our bunks. I do remember a torch in the face and a voice saying "That's him" and I went back to sleep.

06:45 Call the hands was followed some time later by RO's Perkins, McLean and Bailey report to the Master At Arms office. Big shouts of laughter round the mess and enquiries about what we had done wrong this time. I hadn't got a scooby doo until our Joss showed us the 4-page statement Mr Aylott had scribed the night before. Naming all 3 of us as verbally abusing him and civilian passengers (which was a stretch of the truth). I certainly did not abuse Mr Aylott. The charge (in my case) was a travesty, to which I maintain my innocence in that part. However, a Joss's word clearly outranks anything a scabby ab can say.

Officer Of the Day Table later that day. I suggested no plea as this was clearly going up to the Commanders Table (experience has some benefits). How do you plead? Was the standard question. Bailey said "Not guilty", McLean followed suit and I thought shit, they must have found an angle, so went "Not guilty" as well. On caps march out. "So what's the angle?" I asked my Irish and Scottish colleagues? To which came the eloquent and carefully thought through argument "Fuck em, they are not getting me on a trumped up charge!" I did think WTF...... but the circus continued the following day(s) when the Commander (definitely not my friend) had us march into his table.

Off caps. Charge read out. Our pleas stated. The XO then asks what the hell were the "inane mumblings" reported by MAA Aylott. I replied that we were doing excerpts from Monty Python's flying circus. "I don't like Monty Pythons Flying Circus" shouted the Commander peering down at us. Then came the bombshell. As we had pleaded not guilty, we had to have MAA Aylott appear to give evidence and we were at sea. So was the Achilles. So, until both ships could be together, we were on stoppage of leave. On caps, march out. Fuck.

Jumbo, our killick Reg (Leading Regulator) informed us it would be at least a month before both ships were together, for the naval review on the Solent. Fuck. And then of course we would be found guilty and have to take the punishment. Better to bite the bullet and take what's coming now was his suggestion and uppermost in my thoughts. Stoppage of leave, is after all, a punishment in itself. Though it did take a couple of cans of beer and a fag or two to persuade Bailey and McLean but I did.

We went to see Jumbo first and explained that we wanted to change our plea and he helped us to word a suitable argument about seeing the error of our ways. We got a good going over at the table. 14 days No.9's and 14 days stoppage of leave. Which meant we never got onto dry land before the review commenced and missed out on some epic runs ashore by all accounts.

However, we had “Seadays” and “Families Day” before the big Royal Navy Review. Something different to look forward to.

Sea Days was a public-relations, business development and recruitment extravaganza over a three or four-day period. Four or five warships, laden down with civilian VIP’s made up of local authority leaders, university students, central government officials from the Ministry of Defence and the like. Each ship had anywhere between 50 and 150 civilians onboard. Picked up from Pompey.

We sailed out into the Solent and the English Channel and played “War” for them. Firing guns, being strafed by Buccaneer and Phantom jets from the RN airbases ashore, submarine attacks and the small flotilla of fast patrol boats came whizzing in dropping smoke and stuff. Lots of thunder flashes etc. it was quite exciting for the uninitiated.

The last day of the week was given over to “Families Day” all the same action but for our loved ones to experience. I had told my Mum and Dad what was on offer. All they had to do was get down to Portsmouth for an early boarding and day at sea. The original plan was for me to then return home with them for the weekend and get a single train back on the Sunday. However, I was now in the shit and would not be able to do so.

Dad decided to make the journey down from Stockport with Ged, who was excited to get on his big brother’s ship. I had to explain that it wasn’t my ship but I just worked on it. Semantics, I know. Dad couldn’t afford to stay in a hotel or bed and breakfast, so his plan was simple. He dropped the back seats in his Ford Cortina estate and filled the void with a double inflatable mattress they went camping with and take a couple of sleeping bags for him and Ged.

Dad drove down and stopped in a lay bye overnight. Got up early to have a wash and shave in a service station toilets, then drove into the dockyard and parked in the visitor bays that had been set up. I had to “sign” for them when they got onboard. I showed them where I slept in the mess we lived in, the MCO, the dining hall etc. as we did provide lunch. Then we got to sea.

Dad wanted to go on the bridge and Ged wanted to see the helicopter. I left Dad in the care of my oppo Bilbo and took Ged aft with the strict instructions not to touch anything.

We got to the arse end and there was inevitably a queue of people wanting to see the chopper and the WAFU's were all aglow in the moment. Ged decided to grab one of the wheels and got covered in grease just as the little WAFU chain was lifting him up and both he and his oppo inside the crate got a couple of green grease handprints on their sparklingly clean white fronts. Sorry shippers.

Ged was in his element and got to wear a crewman's helmet and headset, whilst sat in the pilot's seat fiddling with the joystick and controls, thankfully all turned off.

On the way back to the bridge I showed Ged the 20mm cannon and the flagdeck. When I got to the bridge I couldn't see Dad and gestured a "where is he?" to Bilbo, who had a headset on carrying out Tactical Signalling communications with the rest of the flotilla and just pointed up towards the hallowed ground of the upper bridge. Gods domain.

The skipper was in command and sat in the driving seat (no steering wheel) with the Officer of the Watch stood beside him and my Dad stood behind him, arms clasped behind his back whistling "For a life on the ocean wave" and I stood there horrified.

No-one was ever allowed up there. We could tap on the stair to attract attention but the only time ratings were allowed up there was to clean it.

The skipped turned to me with a half-smile on his face. And the mini-conversation, in half sentences went something like this:

Skipper: gently nodding backwards "Your Dad"

Moz: a quiet "Yes Sir"

Skipper: "Time to show him something else?"

Moz: "of course Sir" nodding like mad

Skipper: no words just a gracious gentle sweep of his hand

Moz: "Dad" reaching up and gently tugging his coat "time to go"

Skipper: "Thank you"

Moz: pulling Dad firmly away from the bridge and trying to explain to Dad..... we don't go up there

I got him back to the flagdeck and the Commander was pacing out onto the bridge wing. My mate. Dad pointed and asked if that was the guy who had put me on stoppage of leave. I said it was. Dad was only going to walk over and have a chat about letting me home for the weekend and delaying my pun a week..... FFS Dad, this is the navy. There are no allowances like that. I am in the shit.

When we docked, Dad, Ged and all the other families went home, as did those without duty or pun. Not me, I had to turn to.

Once I was in the shit, I was singled out for attention. My pit was the one opened in evening rounds to reveal underwear drying on the roll bar. My locker keys were "discovered" in my unattended locker when I got up for a shit in the middle of the night and other things resulting in more 9's. To be honest, I cannot quite remember all the punishment periods and what they were for. There certainly were a fair few.

I had to go on a "be good all the time" period which was very difficult. I worked hard at it. I was also progressing in my capability and RS George Bullyment suggested I take my LRO Professional Qualifying Examination. Which required a request going up the chain. Nice to get to a table without having to remove my cap.

When asked by the Commander on who was recommending the request, Lt. Leonard our SCO read out the request for Perkins to have permission to take his professional examination. The Commander shouted "I wouldn't recommend this man to be a monkeys uncle! I will not hear a request until this rating has at least 6 months good conduct. Now march him out!" I marched out to a queue of defaulters and other would be requesters falling about in stitches... Cue monkey sounds following me around for a few weeks afterwards....

It was hard work being good for 6 months but at least I had a start. And so I managed 6 months good conduct. I had my request approved and was able to take the examination. Which I promptly failed....

It would be another year before I could retake the exam. 6 months wait in between, plus 3 months for the exam and by then we were in refit and I missed my chance on the Antrim.

Staying out of trouble meant not getting caught and I began to get a lot better at not getting caught but things still happened and being me, I was never going to take a step backwards and always stood my ground.

One of my mates was Jamie Stewart, a not-so-tall jock from Glenrothes who was just like me. Always had something to say and wasn't slow in coming forward. In Defence Watches, we were opposite numbers, taking over from each other and ensuring continuity. He started bringing me a brew and a piece of toast when I had to get up for the 0800 watch after the slaughter of the previous day ending at 0200 and feeling like death warmed up. So I returned the gesture. Saved going down the canteen to grab some grub and probably shaved ten minutes off, meaning a few more Zeds could be laid down.

We went ashore together when we could and always had time for each other. We are still in contact and I play Scrabble Go with him most days, despite the geographical distance (and gaps in time) between us. We are still mates.

The routine on nights was the middle watch 0001-0400, would tune up any radio frequencies needed for the following days activities, and route them to wherever they needed to be. Helo control, Operations Room Primary Warfare Officer, the bridge and such like, along with whatever we would need next day in the MCO.

The morning watch 0400-0800 did all the cleaning. Sweeping up, dusting down and mopping out the comms rooms, CCR, UHF and MCO. Making the place look nice and tiddly for the daytime when the non-watch keepers woke up.

So I got a shout Moz go and check out the Ops Room frequencies they cannot talk to whoever. So off I go down to the CCR, the heart of all the distribution network and our new watch sprog Danny Cousins jogs along with me. When I got into the CCR, I look at the days COMPLAN and noted that it hadn't been changed during the middle and then found another. So like any good matelot, I began "chinning" or whinging about people not doing the job they were supposed to do. It was like a chant, swear at Jamie whilst tuning the radio's up as quick as I could, as I still had to do my share of the cleaning.

Coming off the Morning watch, you go straight to breakfast, scoff a load as quick as you can then get back to the mess and hope the floor is dry so you can crawl into your pit for another 30 minutes of Zeds. So there I am leaning on the door willing the floor tiles to dry when Jamie walks past going to the heads, looking pretty rough as he has only had about 3 hours sleep and has to turn to until lunchtime before he can hit his pit.

Danny then regales my outbursts during the Morning watch about how I was going to give Jamie Stewart a good kicking. I thought wearily for fuck sake Danny and turned to Jamie to explain that it was all in the moment and he turned to face me and immediately stated that I was full of shit whilst touching his fingers to his thumb rapidly demonstrating that I talk too much, so punched him full in the face and he fell backwards into the flat by the heads with me leaping on him and both of us throwing punches.

Cue everyone in the vicinity, including those cleaning out the heads and our messmates to separate two snarling figures. Unchecked I guess we would have fought it out properly but were despatched our ways. Him to the bog and me to my pit.

We didn't see each other the rest of the day. After lunch he got his head down and I had to turn to cleaning, painting or polishing something. The first time we did was in the evening during the dog watches and I was sat in the mess square when he came in. I did the right thing and bought him a can of beer and apologised. By the time we had two or three cans we had decided to batter Danny Cousins… haha. We never did. I am still in touch with Danny via Facebook and did meet him for a beer in Kuala Lumpur when I was on holiday there in 2018. Great lads.

There were a number of different duties and tasks that all of us were required to undertake. I did my stint as Scullery Party, cleaning other peoples shit. Which was putting the steel dining trays and cutlery into a steam cleaner and dryer, stacking them up for the next diners. Wiping down the tables, sweeping and mopping out the dining hall. All under the wind up shouts of "Clean my shit!"….

We all had primary, secondary and tertiary ships duties as well. If you were on duty as a Radio Operator when Action Stations sounded, that is where you needed to be. If I was off-watch, my secondary duty was Layer and Loader for the 20mm Oerlikon Gun and my tertiary role was fire-fighting and damage control.

For a time we also had a night shift who were responsible for heavy cleaning of the heads and bathrooms, along with painting sections that had high footfall in the daylight hours. I am not sure what their official title was but they called themselves MAFRO. The Messdecks and Flats Resistance Organisation.

Their presence was evidenced the following day, with the word MAFRO under the polish they had laid or the screen they had painted. It wasn't obvious and you had to stand in the right light to see it but it was a funny thing. They would scrub down the floor. Paint MAFRO with strokes of a brush one way. Let it dry, then paint the surface at 90 degree's. As I say, you had to know what they were doing.

One of the lads was very, very tall. Too tall for a ship really. I nicknamed him Bus Stop.

During the middle and morning watches, radio operators were forever tracking backwards and forwards between the MCO on 2 deck and the CCR on 1 deck at the end of the long passageway with senior rates messes either side and the NAAFI shop, which had a little set back for a side entry door. This is where MAFRO crashed out and got their heads down and the big guy who could never sleep, was stood inside the set back but would periodically slowly stick his head out to see if anyone in authority was coming, then it was his job to kick them all awake and look alive. To me walking along the dimly lit passageway and seeing his head come out reminded of someone stood at a bus stop peering out for the next bus. Magic.

We had a problem when some bright spark left a rag in their bucket after mopping out and slung it into a trap, which was the usual routine but instead of pulling out the rag washing his hands, he must have just pressed the flush and off it disappeared.

Unlike the normal sewer and waste-water drainage ashore, at sea it needed to be helped on its way through a vacuum system by a flush of high-pressure water. Not usually a problem and capable of managing even the most hardy of branches that a matelot may shit out.

However, this must have been one rag too many as it stopped up the filter located down below in the bilges and backed up, with spectacular results. All 8 traps surcharged back all the shit, piss and shiny bog roll (we never had any soft stuff) back up into the heads with a massive WHOOSH!

I didn't see the it but was detailed as one of two "volunteers" from each forward mess to create a working party to support the not-very-happy chippies who had to sort out the blockage. Our role was to scoop up the shit. I kid you not.

Rig of the day for the exercise was minimal clothing as it was going to get covered in shit, so there we are in skidders (to hold the tackle in place and for limited modesty) and flip flops with dustpans and buckets scraping up the sludge. It stunk to high heaven and was not for the faint hearted. It took some time. Then we had to scrub out and wipe down the bulkheads, trap doors etc. before mopping out and then got time off to shower. Thoroughly.

Daily Orders covered the issue and instructed people to be sensible and avoid repeating the exercise. Now I don't know much about auto-suggestion or the psychology of copycat stuff but guess what, it happened again and again. Thankfully having done the work once, the cleaning task befell others on each occasion. A proper twat of a clean up job.

The XO decreed that we would therefore "guard" the heads during mess cleaning, in the morning and evening and so it happened. A duty was created, split across the three forward messes, to provide someone to check the buckets of murky water being poured down the traps in the heads to ensure no further blockages. I shit you not. It went on for pretty much the rest of that particular trip.

Jack gets bored at sea with the challenge of exercises or getting ashore and so will get up to all sorts of antics onboard. Probably the funniest was the saga of the "Phantom Giggler" and the result of many weeks of exercises and Defence Watches with the creation of the "NFI club" or better known as the Not Fucking Interested club. Complete with little badges awarded when you had done something of significance to demonstrate that you weren't interested in doing something.

Rocky had a bandana with NFI on the front, which he wore on middle and morning watches in the MCO. We put little stickers on every piece of equipment in the MCO, tiny things stuck inside that read "This kit is NFI" and giggled about it. A very childish prank that only those in the know, really knew about it.

However, it didn't get past the skipper once he asked a bunting what the little NFI badge was and blew his top when he found out. An instruction immediately went round all departments and it appeared on Daily Orders that anyone displaying any form of it would be disciplined. So all the kit was cleaned, badges destroyed and almost all traces of it disappeared. Almost all.

Someone had scratched (inverted) onto one of the Ormig reproduction rollers in the MCO that only appeared in the corner of a signal and so faint it was barely readable. An ingenious move that read "this signal is NFI"

No-one sussed it at all, that was until FOF1 boarded and it was the two and half ringed Flag Senior Communications Officer, a largely redundant role in my humble opinion, as we already had one for the ship, why did we need two. So it was no surprise that he spent a lot of his time on a quality control drive when he was with us. This must have included scrutinising each signal as he noticed the little smudge in the corner of one signal and produced a fucking magnifying glass from his pocket and peered at the signal. Then looked up.

The MCO was going like a chippy on a Friday night, with signals inbound and outbound appearing every minute or so and the head of the watch was LRO Vic Flynn, a large bearded and laconic salt who rarely had time for anything and he is proof reading a very urgent signal that a sparker is waiting anxiously to despatch.

The Flag SCO stands in front of Vic and the conversation goes something like this

Flag SCO: "LRO?" in that upper-class questioning tone demanding instant attention

Vic Flynn: "Just a moment Sir" not looking up

Flag SCO: "L-R-O?" he spells out

Vic Flynn: "I just need a moment Sir, I have a Flash signal to go now" still not looking up

The Flag SCO bangs his fist on the signal that Vic is reading to get his attention and Vic looks up at him and fixes him with a steely gaze "Yes Sir"

"What is NFI and why is it on the corner of this signal?" demands the Flag SCO

Vic keeps a straight face and firmly pulls the signal he was verifying from under the Flag SCO's fist to pass to the sparker for transmission and became a legend overnight when he replied "I don't know Sir, I am not fucking interested really" and the whole MCO full of six radio operators collapsed in fits of laughter.

The SCO made a stormy exit, presumably to clarify what he had discovered with our own SCO Lt. Leonard whilst the bunting on duty scrambled to disconnect the reproducer and replace the roll inside with a new one.

The "Phantom Giggler" was far more anarchic though and pretty much a direct piece of insubordination that was made totally public and must have been humiliating for the skipper. I am not sure when it started, it certainly would not have been during an exercise and probably the result of too much time on the hands of the perpetrator.

A pipe is an all-ship voice broadcast and used to alert the ships company to something important enough for everyone to know at the same time. There were some standard ones like Call The Hands at 06:45 when all the community lighting was switched off. Sometimes accompanied by a dit which may be Call The Hands, Call The Hands, Call The Hands. Short gap followed by "Hands off cocks and pull on your socks" or the more satire of "Stop Sleeping" a particular favourite of mine.

Other pipes may be a warning that Helo is taking off or landing, when it could and for all hands to stay clear of the flight deck and other such operational data, like commencing officer of the watch manoeuvres. This would be when he would sling the ship into a series of tight turns designed to send your can of beer or mug of tea sideways across whichever flat surface was available to leave it, in that moment, before dousing some other unfortunate in beer or a hot drink. The pipe was merely a warning to take control of your errant drink.

Anyway, on one particular day after an operational pipe had been made someone, with access to a microphone, emitted a loud and very long giggle. It was hilarious. Everyone fell about laughing and so it began.

The giggles followed the Skippers daily pipe and every operational pipe for days. It got to be disappointing if there wasn't one and the guy doing it was clever, he didn't giggle after every one of them. He may have been on watch somewhere else but either way it was pretty ad-hoc.

The skipper, clearly not happy, had called his senior technical team around him and located every single microphone on the ship that could be used to make a ship-wide broadcast. Satisfied that he had covered all the angles, the skipper made his daily announcement on what we were doing etc. and said confidently that we would hear nothing more from the phantom giggler. He said "Out" as the usual indication his speech had finished when the phantom giggler let out a particularly long and loud giggle.

This brought the house down. I am sure even the officers were laughing, we certainly were down below and up top, wherever we were. It was funny. It was, however, also hugely embarrassing for the command and a serious breach of discipline and it had to be stopped.

The skipper organised a complete trace of every communication line throughout the ship and it was discovered that a microphone had been wired into the voice comms cable that passed the bunk of one of the Communications Electrical Mechanics (CEM), who had clearly recognised the opportunity and took full advantage. I am not sure of his ultimate fate but he got chucked off the Antrim and things settled down until the next opportunity to be anarchic...

It wasn't always full on exercises and repeated practice fire-fighting and damage control, operating the ship and maintaining all its moving and fixed parts, there were sometimes a bit of down time and none more so odd than "Hands to Bathe"

"Hands to bathe!" is the pipe that spawns a mad dash to grab your shorts and jump overboard from a perfectly serviceable (and floating nicely) warship. Usually hundreds of miles from the shore and often in the breeding grounds of great white sharks, or other dangerous things.

Protected only by a couple of SLR toting bridge marksmen and an inflatable crewed by grinning Sterling sub-machine handling fellow matelot's.

I "bathed" in the deep blue of the Pacific on another ship later in my career but it was the Caribbean, the grey Atlantic and the greeny blue Mediterranean Sea that I swam in from the Antrim. Later on, I bathed in the grey and harsh North Sea, which froze my proverbial's into shrivelled walnuts and nearly gave me a heart attack!

Why did we do it? Because we could.

Early in 1977 we had trips to Hamburg and Copenhagen after exercising with NATO ships in the Baltic, both eagerly anticipated as being the home for the discerning pornographic culture so sought after by lonely matelot's at sea.

Once alongside and those who could go ashore as the gangway landed and permission was given, advanced at great speed in the search for a porny movie house. Others would head for the lady's of the night who also operated in the daytime incidentally, as we all sought satisfaction in our various ways.

2E Mess went ashore as a team, like we always did, mob handed. It was one of those days when we had to practice the endless go ashore game of "Losing Lennie" and it chucked up many innovative methods as no-one wanted to end up in a bar drinking with him. To add spice to the game, Lennie knew we would be trying to lose him and he adopted all sorts of schemes to stay with the biggest group he could.

We were stretched out along a road wandering round the red-light district and Lennie had strategically placed himself in the middle, this meant he kept his options open to the maximum degree. For those at the back, it was pretty easy to peel away and head off for pastures new as they were now Lennie-less.

Lennie looked back in alarm and scuttled forward to overtake people and resume his place in the middle of the now diminishing pack and it was really getting down to the wire and I had no intention of ending up drinking with him as I, like most of the mess, didn't like his company.

I think we had been pared down from about a dozen to just 6 and it was becoming increasingly difficult but my oppo Gaz Richardson from Coventry who used to box a bit, had other ideas.

As we crossed the road to peer into a sex shop through the window blinds to see what they had on offer inside, something kinky perhaps. A massive articulated lorry came down the road effectively splitting the pair of us off from Lennie and the remaining three. Gaz grabbed my arm and dragged me through the next door, which was a shadowy pub and dragged me to the back of the room to a corner spot at the bar.

The lorry passed and the remaining three plus Lennie searched hopelessly up the street. They must have gone into the sex shop first, as that is where they last saw us and at some point peered into the bar and Gaz just instructed me to freeze. So I did.

They didn't come in the bar, the mugs, ha ha and wandered off with Lennie to drink themselves into oblivion. Losing Lennie was played by our mess in every port we went to when he was onboard and by the way, he still had a small dick.

Gaz and I took on the role of beer bosun in 77 after a period of steady losses in mess funds to the point where we didn't have enough money to go and buy our allocation of beer from the NAAFI. Horrifying.

It came to a head when the ever so popular (not) Harry Lauder (by name and nature) a loud mouthed West Ham fan who used to get angrier the more he drank, opened the fridge lock with a butter knife one day and I realised then why there was no money in the kitty. People had been helping themselves to "free" beer.

During a loud and angry mess meeting, Gaz and I took on the job as long as we could get the fridge banded with steel and put a hasp and padlock on it. So we did.

Within weeks we were turning a profit back in and were able to pay back the investors their stake and continue to provide a bank for loans and stuff. Mess funds were traditionally divvied up at the end of a big trip, in our case when we got back from the WINDIES for Christmas.

We were paid fortnightly, in cash, in your hand when you paraded to receive your wages. Name shouted out, you step forward, paybook extended from your left hand, whilst saluting and stating your official number. Your fortnightly pay was then slapped into your paybook and you stepped smartly away.

A wallet full of cash you were a lord for a week. Spending money on beer and women and generally enjoying yourself. However, the following week, also known as a "blank week" with no incoming pay, a matelot would become a miser and hold onto his last beer chits as long as possible. Some, however, fell to the lure of going ashore and needed more money.

This is where mess funds came in. It was our little bank. You could borrow money at 10% interest per week. All recorded in a little book held by the banker. So a tenner would require a payment of eleven pounds back to the bank on pay day. Some lads were always borrowing. I never did. We invested a stake at the start of the trip and got that back, plus a share of the "profits" at the end of the trip. In my case I was £54 up going home for chrimbo.

1977 was Silver Jubilee year and the Antrim had the pleasure of being the royal guardship on the Caribbean tour. We had some great runs ashore all over the West Indies. Bermuda, the Bahamas (both Nassau and Freeport), Tortola, Antigua and many others. Certainly my most favourite part of the world. All the time I was drawing cartoons and helping to create the daily paper.

FORY (Flag Officer Royal Yacht) was a mate of our skipper and had seen a copy of the ship's newspaper. He in turn or at the same event, showed a copy to Prince Phillip, who also thought it was a good thing and something that HRH would like to see.

At the end of the tour, we ran into Barbados with the Royal Yacht and there was a well -choreographed and photographed flypast with a Concorde that was there to pick up the royal party and convey them to the UK to continue the silver jubilee celebrations.

At some point that morning, there was a pipe "RO1 Perkins, Bridge" nothing else. Not a normal summons for Moi but off I trotted to meet my fate.

The skipper called me up to the upper bridge (the inner sanctum) and explained about FORY and Prince Phillip and instructed me to produce a souvenir edition of the Antrim News for HRH The Queen.

It had to have a normal topical front cover and clean. A risqué but clean page 3 and a very clean and topical crossword. He said that he needed it by the time we berthed alongside in Bridgetown. Off I went and proper scratched my head.

During the entire tour, we had been accosted by numerous yank tourists all keen to know more about the Queen. Responding to repeated questions of "Are you on the Royal Yacht?" and we would say no, we are on the Antrim. "What's that?" they would say and immediately lose attention and move away. It was a tad disrespectful to us and a little irritating.

So when the Concorde flew over, I knew I had the front page. The rest of the guys turned up trumps with their elements of the paper and attached to this post is the front cover. Sadly I do not have a full copy of that edition but hopefully it will make you smile and remember, plus the one when Mr Webb fixed the broken chopper. I think I could have but have never really, added "by royal appointment" to my subsequent cartoons.... Haha.

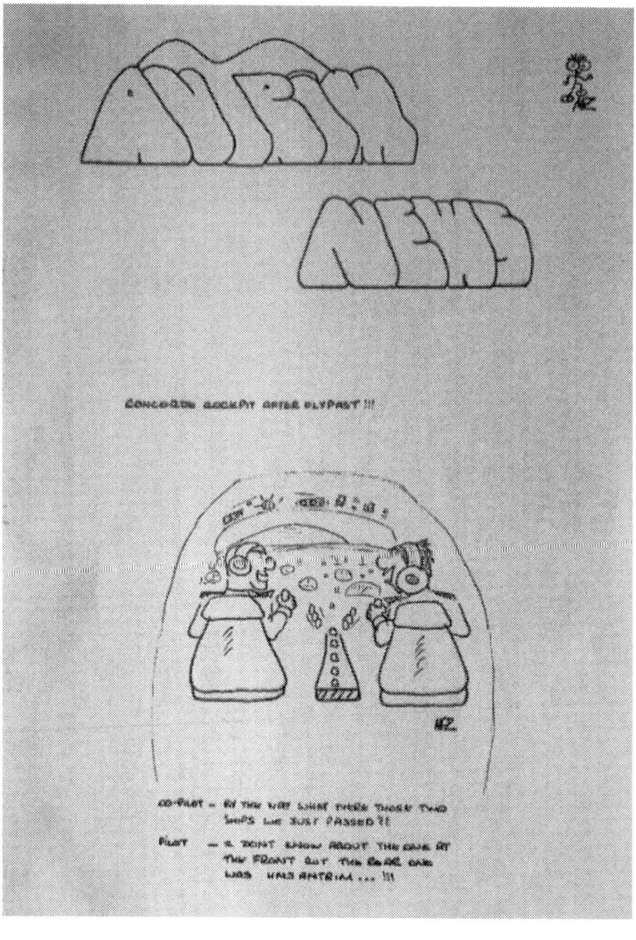

As we sailed across the grey Atlantic, for a refuel in the Azores and an eventual arrival in Pompey in time for people to get away for Chrimbo. One of the days, I had a call from the SCO to meet him at close of play. I did and he escorted me up to the Captains Cabin. I was then asked to stand in a line with some heavyweight (seniority and capability) senior rates and officers.

The skipper came in and greeted us all and then went straight into a series of big thank you and hand-shakes with all and sundry, Chief whoever had spent countless hours fixing the helo, Chief and PO someone had done sterling work keeping the knackered seaslug shipshape and so on, until he came to “scabby ab” Perkins.

“And for all your great work with the ships newspaper and your funny cartoons here is a little thank you from me”. A cheque for a fiver and on a blank week as well. But the really bonus moment was seeing the Commanders red and seething face behind the skipper. He really didn’t like me…..

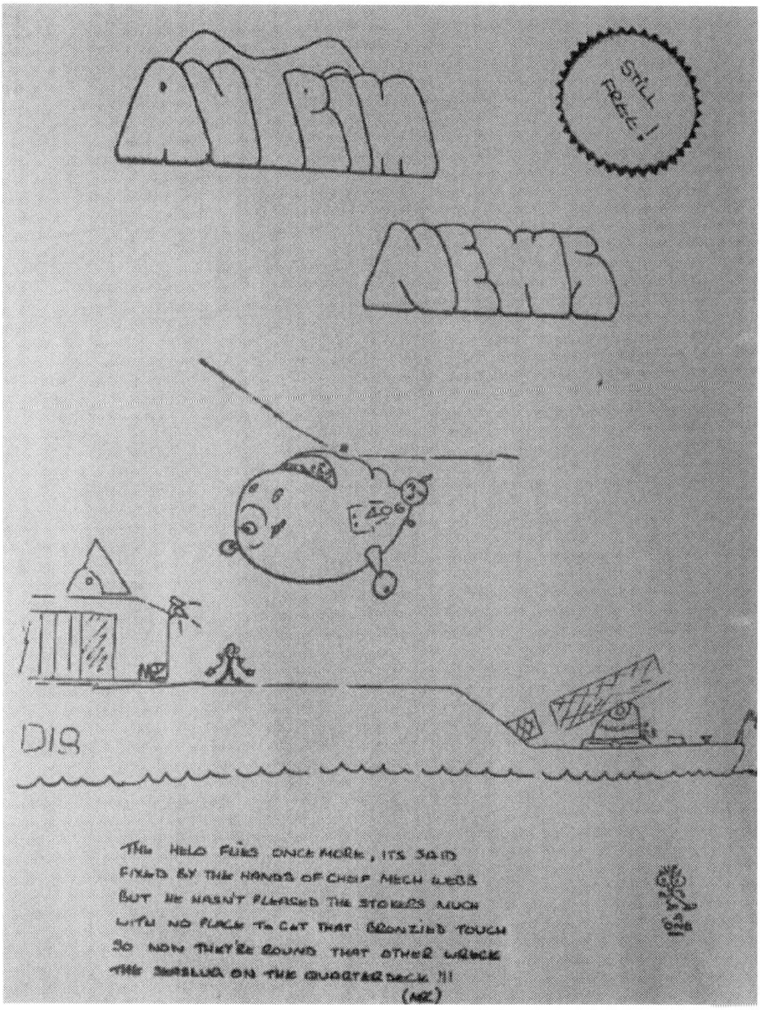

At some point we operated out of Gibraltar for a couple of weeks, acting as guardship and carrying out exercises with passing naval forces. I had got into the ships Internal Security unit, which would be the armed response to anything needed off ship and as a back up to the small detachment of Irish Rangers who went everywhere with us. Bluejackets they called us (a very aged term for armed sailors). Whilst they wore camo dress round the ship. Hard to use their field expertise hiding on a grey hulk but hey, who was I to argue.

We spent some time on the firing ranges at Gib and carried out some exercises and we handled a number of different weapons as part of it. Good fun.

On our last weekend in Gib everyone was busy getting ashore to drink their last beers and I was drinking with a big "dabtoe" that shared our mess, called Bill Jack. We were legless when we got back to the ship for supper and to get changed. This consisted of swapping our beer-soaked t-shirt for a clean one and then we would be back at it.

All the bunks had been lifted. Middle bunks were normally folded up and then down to form the back of seating, using the bottom bunk to sit on. Sprogs had bottom bunks and it wasn't nice climbing into your pit after big hairy arses have been sat on it all evening but that's how it was.

The bunks were folded up and the lad who had the bottom pit below me was a scruffy urchin called Timmins and he was a crab. Several times we had thrown him into the showers and scrubbed him down with wire wool pads but it was to no avail. He always smelled. Bill commented that his pit was up and unzipped, so he pulled the blanket back to show his dirty sheets. So we decided to teach him a lesson.

Bill grabbed a roll of black masking tape and we proceeded to wrap his bunk up from end to end so that it looked like a fat black sausage. We laughed, got changed and went back ashore for more drinks.

I got back late and noted that Timmins the crab had just slit open the masking tape with his knife, which was left on the punka louvre cover next to his bed. Punka louvres were the only way of bringing any form of fresh air into the mess. Anyway, he was snuggled down inside the tape like a giant chrysalis and I then noticed there was some tape left on the roll.

Bill's bunk was next to mine, end on end. My feet at his head. He had left his skidders and socks to dry on his bunk roll bar, so I thought it would be funny to mould his underwear to the roll bar by sticking the remaining masking tape, wound round and round over it until it was completely covered. Laughing to myself I climbed into my bunk and got my head down.

I awoke suddenly and in pain. My bunk light was on and Bill Jack had woke me by punching me in the face two or three times as my head started to clear I thought I would give it back to him but as he saw me move he pulled up Timmins knife and shoved it in front of my face. Try it and you'll get this he snarled. So I didn't move. He punched me once more and then backed off, still holding Timmins knife but I didn't get out of my bunk.

He got undressed, tossed Timmins knife down, growled a bit at me and climbed into his bunk, turned his light off and fell asleep on his back snoring.

My bunk light was still on and I tried a careful glance round the mess square only to see everyone staring back at me and I thought fuck, I needed to sort out a response now. So I climbed out of bed and limbered up a bit in the mess square and briefly thought through what I was going to do.

I started off with a shout and grabbed Bill by his beard and pulled him upwards to smash his face on the bunk above two or three times, then nutted him in the face, stood back and launched several punches into his face shouting at him never to pull a knife on me again. Then I did the honourable thing and stepped away from his bunk and invited him to stand up and face me in the mess square.

Bill just look shocked and hurt shaking his head. Then he rolled over and faced the buggery board that separated his bunk from his neighbour in the annexe and I calmed myself down as best I could. I glimpsed around the mess and a few nods told me that I had done the right thing. So I climbed back into my pit but kept the sheet and blanket pulled back for a quick escape if Bill decided to go another round but he didn't.

We never drank together again and never once spoke about the incident. He worked a different part of ship so the only time we interacted was in the mess. I got a move to the starboard annex a few months later when Kev Goodall left the ship. A top bunk, out of the way and he left the Antrim. We didn't exchange addresses or wishes to stay in touch.

So I am in my period of "being good" which of course can also be translated into "not getting caught" and I was doing quite well. I was progressing towards taking my Leading Radio Operator (General) Professional Qualifying Examination and life was good.

I had a new girl friend back home in Stockport. Anne from Cale Green, a very bright girl. Lots of O and A levels from her time at the convent school (genuine) who liked a drink, who loved sex and had tattoo's on her arms, hands and knuckles. Whilst its all the rage these days, it was not quite the common thing in the 70's, plus hers were all home-made.

My Mum loved her to bits (not in any way, at all, or ever) but Moz was seeding his oats on a regular basis, interspersed with lots of drinking and both vertical and horizontal dancing. Life was good. Her mum was pretty direct and didn't really take to me, her drug-taking brother had a bed setee in the front room but apart from a couple of beers in the pub to celebrate her Mum's birthday with him once, I didn't like him at all and didn't engage with him. There was no Dad around and occasionally when her Grandad wasn't well, he moved in and took Anne's bedroom. He was referred to as the "Old Bugger". She then shared a bed with her Mum and I wouldn't be able to stay overnight. There was never any mention of a three-some.

I would come home on a weekend, drop off my bag of dirty clothes with my Mum and, get bathed and shaved and be off for a 36-hour alcohol fuelled sexathon with Anne. We had some good laughs and many solid pub crawls. Everything a young matelot needed in one package. She could match me for drinking and took a lead in the bedroom.

Anne had written to me the week before I came home, explaining that as her Grandad was ill and I would not be able to stay over. All I could think of was this hampered things, in the sex department but I was sure we could work around it. So I got there on Friday evening. Brother was out. Mother was watching television and there was a tall carriage case clock, a trunk and some other things that I didn't recognise cluttering up the front room. I was sat on the sofa next to her Mother in an icy silence, watching some drivel on the goggle box and I thought I would try and start a conversation at least.

Looking round at the additional furniture, I said "Has the Old Bugger moved in again?" and her Mother burst into tears. Anne came running downstairs and shouted at me as to what I had said. I shared and she revealed that he had died and these things had been recovered from his flat. I just needed a hole to fall down into but it didn't materialise. It wasn't the most sociable of evenings and I ended up back at home by myself and didn't get a shag.

Anne worked at the Alma Lodge in housekeeping. Sundays to Thursday's which meant we had Friday's and Saturday's to do as we like. She had to be in work for 06:45 on a Sunday morning, so I would be up and about shortly afterwards to spend the rest of Sunday with the family, then get a lift to the railway station to commence the long trip back down to Portsmouth

One of the Sunday mornings I was at the bottom of the stairs (centrally located in a 2-up, 2-down terraced house and I could hear her brother snoring in the room next to me. I was just straightening my united scarf into a muffler and about to zip up my leather bomber jacket, when both front and back doors exploded inwards with an almighty crash and the house was suddenly filled with big hairy arsed coppers who pounced on me and Anne's dodgy brother in his bed setee.

I was bundled to the floor, hands cuffed behind me and arrested. Then I was dragged out and thrown non-too-ceremonially into the back of a car, which screeched away whilst I was still getting my head in gear. It was a fairly decent effort to cure a hangover for sure as my mind raced along all permutations of what may have happened and why I was caught up in something I hadn't a clue about.

I got shoved into an interview room with two detectives. No charge desk, no offer of legal representation. Moi, the clothes I was stood in, my wallet, fags and a lighter. The coppers started firing questions at me about when did I break into the Chemist's and where are the drugs? Despite me saying that I was at home for the weekend and a serving member of HM Armed Forces. I even flashed my ID card to them, which one of them snatched out of my hand to stare at.

I explained that I was on HMS Antrim. Did I have the contact number? Yes I did and read it out. How do you know that? Because one of my duties as a radio operator is to man the ships telephone exchange when alongside.

Are you on the run? No, I am home on leave? Are you sure? What? They were acting out the good cop / bad cop routine and when the bad cop went out to validate my story and I asked very politely not to mention where I was, the good cop starts being all syrupy and telling me he I need to answer the questions truthfully or I would get into real trouble.

Bad cop came back and confirmed he had spoken to the Officer of the Day on the Antrim who verified I wasn't on the run, well I wasn't due back until Monday morning at 06:30, so technically not on the run. Thanks mate and then he continued to question me about a burglary at a chemist shop somewhere in Levenshulme, which of course I knew nothing about.

They put me into a cell and I remained there most of Sunday. They finally let me out mid-afternoon after corroborating I had nothing to do with the burglary, I couldn't have, as I was on the ship at the time of the event. Whether or not Anne's brother had contributed to my story in my defence, I will never know.

Anyway, they de-arrested me and let out of the door. When I realised we were in Cheadle Hulme and it was a long walk to Offerton, I made the difficult financial decision to order a taxi from a call box located nearby. I only ever reverted to taxi's as a last resort as I thought they were the most expensive form of travel. I was used to walking or running everywhere, or getting a bus.

I got home and gave the family a long and winding story about meeting Anne's family and staying for a chat, which although not quite a lie, certainly stretched the truth to snapping point...

Sunday evening I got back on board the Antrim moored out on the jetty's furthest from the dockyard gates was always a long haul and not helped as I walked up the gangway to be greeted by the duty QM saying welcome on board junkie confirmed my suspicions that the event was not going to slip by quietly.

Monday morning call the hands pipe at 06:45 was followed shortly by a very familiar announcement of "RO1 Perkins, Master At Arms office" which always raised a cheer in 2E Mess. So I went to see the Joss for a chat before breakfast.

Joss: "I thought you were being good"

Moz: "I am Sir"

Joss: "Well getting arrested by the Drug Squad in Stockport is not good in my eyes"

Moz: "No Sir"

Joss: "Do you love this girl?"

Moz: "Not really Sir, she is good company and a good squeeze"

Joss: "Do you want a career in the Royal Navy?"

Moz: "Yes Sir"

Joss: "Lose the girl then Perkins?"

Moz: "Aye, aye Sir"

So I did and I did the honourable thing by telling her face to face, in the pub a couple of weeks later. There were some words and a bit of emotion but we all got over it quickly and I left. Shame really, as she had only just had her tattoo's removed for me.

I occasionally see Anne now and then, as she doesn't live that far away from me and we exchange greetings but that is about it. No mention of the past.

I came home once or twice more that spring and dossed about on leave. Had beers with some of my old civvie mates but they were at work and socially we had become quite distanced. Mum instructed our David to introduce me to some of his friends. He was at College at the time and working part time at shoe shop called Curtess.

David said that he and some friends were going out on Friday and invited me to join him. I wasn't too interested until he said there would be two guys and six girls. Suitably impressed by the odds I thought I would join him. We met for drinks in a pub in Didsbury called, The Didsbury. However, the odds thing turned immediately on its head when I met the talent.

Two of them were kids, probably had Saturday jobs and too young for the mature 20-year old that I was, so I ignored them. Two were married, one was a little too old for me and the other was engaged. Realising that my opportunities were limited, I resorted to telling funny stories and dirty jokes. Which generated some laugh's but a lot went misunderstood by civilians.

One of the youngsters tried to engage me by saying that her dad was from Portsmouth, well from Waterlooville just outside of Pompey. She told me she had been in Joanna's on the front in Southsea and I launched into a series of funny stories about it being a clip joint, had sticky carpets and probably embarrassed the young thing.

David gave me a telling off on the drive home for being too raucous and vulgar. That I had upset some of his friend's but I just took it on the chin and put it down to an experience. He didn't invite me to any more gathering's and I returned to sea.

Early in 1978 the Antrim needed to go into refit. A massive exercise where every moving part of the ship is taken out to be maintained or replaced with something newer. All parts of ship are chipped down to the bare steel and the exercise of building up sufficient layers of rust preventing paint can be applied. 1 coat of lead oxide, 2 coats of grey undercoat and then 2 coats of grey topcoat.

Chipping paint off came in two methods of work at the time. A single chipping hammer, like a thick chisel head that is continually pounded against the ship until the paint chips off in small and very small pieces. A very monotonous action of raising the hammer and bringing it down in the general area of attention. Keep chipping away until you see shiny steel.

Gloves, goggles and ear defenders as the noise could be quite hellish. Not necessarily from a small group of matelot's chipping away but the Jason Hammers as well. Crude combinations of tungsten steel rods contained in a metal tube, resembling the end of a fire hose but instead of water, compressed air was fired up into the tube from a long hose that caused significant vibration in the steel tube which was then held against the steel in a noisy "BBRRRRPPPPPP, BBBRRRRRPPPPPPPPPPP" sending showers of tiny flakes of paint off in all directions.

A shitty job but we made good progress on the ships sides that were our responsibility, the flag deck, forward screens, forward mast, forward funnel and the bridge. We completed our assigned task and the paint shone. Smooth without any obvious overlaps. A really good job. Our work party was under Dave Woods the Chief Yeoman, who wasn't happy at all.

You cant have finished. Well we had. He said if we have finished, we would have to go and work on some other part of the ship under someone else and fair old convinced us, it would be in our best interests to chip it all off and do it again. WTF.... So we did. However, the second job was never as good as the first, it looked a proper pigs ear to be honest.

It was years later that I worked out Dave Woods concern. It wasn't that we would be working for another department but that he would not have a cushy job watching us chip and paint and get sent somewhere else. He needed something to be in charge of. Slippery bastard. So he kept us painting and re-painting the same sections of ship.

At some point in the refit, a portion of the ships company has to provide shore support to the wider naval base and Debbie and I got drafted out into Buffers Party in Nelsons Barracks and a bit of a culture shock.

Before the refit we had to indicate whether to go into Nelson Barracks or take a Ration Allowance (RA) and live ashore in civvy digs. Some lads without seniority had no choice and had to go into barracks where they had pay stopped to cover food and accommodation. Those on RA were paid £6 a day to live ashore. Hey hey. A commercial opportunity.

Take cheap digs, must less than the allowance and it left you with additional beer chits. A good move. Debbie was humping Angie, a barmaid from our "local" the Mucky Duck (real name The White Swan) and using his RA to supplement her rent. I shared a bedsit with Kev Lowe a very skinny brummie Wolves fan. A few others had digs around us in Southsea and we used to gather in the evenings in a scruffy bar underneath the Queens Hotel or kick a ball about on Southsea Common.

Buffers Party did all the odd jobs around Nelson Barracks but our primary function was to sweep the roads and we called ourselves Wombles. We had little trucks that we pulled along that held three dustbins, a collection of brushes and shovels.

We had to turn to at 07:30 when the rest of base didn't put in an appearance until 08:00. The early start was to sweep the road from the gatehouse to the main block so that when the Admiral, Commander-in-Chief, Naval Home Command (CINCNAVHOME) arrived in his chauffer driven limo, the road was clean and he could see matelots working. Though we didn't work when he came past because we had to stand to attention, so it probably defeated the object of looking like we were working but that's what we had to do.

Sweeping the roads, picking up rubbish from the admin blocks and taking them to the dump. Some proper crappy jobs.

One sunny day we had to paint all the little dust trucks as they were showing wear. Grey bodies and black wheels, black towing handle. So we pimped them up a bit by white walling the tyres and painting Womble Wagon 1, 2, 3 etc. on the trucks in white stencil. They looked great as we wheeled them around and got a few nods of acknowledgement and cheers from the boys, that was until the Admiral spotted them.

A quick repaint in all grey and all black was the result. Cheers Sir. Wipe the smiles off the faces then. Thank you. Doffs cap, scrapes shoes in backward retreat.

The Buffers leading hand, a proper old salt with a family ensconced in the married quarters over on the big Rowner estate in Gosport ran a penny bookmaking club in Buffers Party, open to anyone. He ran a league over 5 days and started the week with 50p in the pot and you had to bet using a maximum of 10p in any day on a variety of horses. Singles, doubles, trebles, accumulators, Yankee's etc. all for a penny a bet.

At the end of the week, whoever won the most points got the pot. It was a bit of fun and appealed to the hardened gamblers. I had done the horses when I worked at Lipton's before I joined the Navy and could follow the form and so joined in.

At different parts of the week and depending on workload the Killick would let you thin out (meaning thinning the remaining group down by leaving) mid-morning. He was fair and shared it out across the team each week.

The Buffer picked Debbie and me for special duties one morning and took us off the killick mid-morning. We had to haul a womble wagon over to Rodney Block which was a disused accommodation block built by the Victorians and out of use for decades. We took full notice of the dangerous building and due for demolition signs by walking straight past them following the Buffer and hauling three dustbins.

The Buffer took us into the middle of the ground floor. The floorboards on the second floor had rotted through and were piled all around the edges of the ground floor leaving a vast open space and a view up to the broken roof, which had spars hanging down and almost no roof tiles. The space was now inhabited by a million shitehawks made up of different species of pigeon, seagull and whatever but just shitehawks to us.

Their excrement, I now know to be called "Guano" is the accumulated excrement of seabirds and bats, was about six inches deep on the floor. As a manure, guano is a highly effective fertilizer due to its exceptionally high content of nitrogen, phosphate and potassium, key ingredients for plant growth and most helpful down at the Buffers allotment where he had a deal selling it to his allotment society friends.

It also causes a variety of respiratory diseases but it was okay for us as the Buffer had brought lengths of cotton sheeting strips to bind over our mouths and noses. Health & Safety at work. Brilliant. The guano layer showed signs of shovelling in the past, so I guess we weren't the first and probably not the last to do the dirty work for the Buffer.

It had a full on ammonia smell and was difficult to fill the 3 bins and tough to then haul them round the back of the buffers store where we needed help to lift them up and into the Buffers trailer and stretch a canvas cover over it. We got thinned out very early that day.

One morning, we are all having a brew after the frenetic effort of sweeping the approach roads was complete and the Killick was calling the bets in. I was still studying form and couldn't really decide what to do with the 5 horses I fancied and I was being hurried up by the Killick. He snatched the paper off me and looked at the ones I had pencilled and began to deride my selection announcing that they were all donkeys.

Debbie was saying farewell as he had been stood down and was off for another shag with Angie in Summerstown across the way and I bridling with anger. I therefore, held him back and told him to put a bet on with me at the bookies. That's how good I thought my selection was, I announced. Everyone laughed as I gave Debbie £2.70, the cheapest stake I could bet on a 5-horse "Canadian"

The Canadian consisted of 26 x 10p bets, 10 doubles, 10 trebles, five four-fold wagers and one five-fold accumulator. Plus, 10p tax.

The team continued to take the piss out of me all morning until I got away mid-afternoon. Giving Debbie the £2.70 restricted my travel options, so instead of the bus I had to walk.

Stomping down Osborne Road just past the Queens Hotel and on my way to the salubrious surroundings of my bedsit on Shaftesbury Road I spotted Debbie sat on a wall at the corner. When he spotted me he jumped up and ran towards me shouting.

He grabbed hold of me and asked me if I knew how long a head was and went "Yer what?" and he again demanded that I answer how long is a horse's head. I said about 3 feet. He said yep. You were 3 feet from several grand. I thought "Oh" but he was still excited and dragged me into the bookies on Osborne Road to point out the winners.

Of course, without my bins my myopic view was a little blurred and I had to squint at the results. I had a winner, a second, a winner, a non-runner and a winner. Hey hey, some money would be coming my way. The non-runner made up a corner of the bets. So, in effect, I had all the benefits of a "Yankee" a 4-horse bet, 6 x doubles, 4 x trebles and a four-fold accumulator. For me this meant a pay-out of about £250, which was an absolute fortune at the time.

I celebrated with Debbie and we went on a proper bender. Drinking all sorts of stuff for the rest of the day and night. I also, very sensibly for me, put a lot of it into my trusty Post Office savings account. I also shared the news of my win and a round of ale, with the Buffers Party the following day. It's always good to share and by doing so, could boast of my betting prowess to the Killick.

Around this time one my oppo's Danny Cousins, a proper ladies man, had ended a relationship with another of the Mucky Ducks finest barmaids Margaret and despite his and others thinking of my best interests and telling me not to, I needed a new squeeze and so we hooked up for a short but rumbustious affair.

Margaret had two of those key qualities a matelot looks for. She loved sex and alcohol. So, with those two boxes ticked I dived in. However, the downside was, she had an irresistible urge to steal things and tell lies, which ultimately led to an angry break up, a storming of the gates and a twist but we will get to that in good time.

I was sharing a bedsit with Kev "Brummie" Lowe in an all-electric flat. We had a fridge but rarely kept much in it, a hob and wall heater, a couple of single beds, drawers and one wardrobe. It wasn't much but it served our needs. All operated off a coin slot meter.

The main bonus was a bed and somewhere for a safe and decent shag. So much better then knee tremblers against walls in the dark. The only problem was sharing a room with an oppo. Sometimes I would give Brummie the nod to go for a walk, sometimes it needed the incentive of 50p to go buy a beer or an ice cream or something, anything to get him out so I could have a shag. Occasionally the moment overtook us and we had a spectator.

We were lay on our respective beds, one evening, Brummie and me, except I had Margaret curled up alongside me on the door-side of the room (Brummie was window-side) and we were watching Sportsnight with David Coleman and the match highlights of some particular teams when Margaret started touching me up.

I glanced over to see Brummie smoking his fags and watching the match highlights and so eased myself onto my side a bit more to give Margaret better access as she played around with me. All the time Brummie is keeping a straight face watching the action, whilst I am getting pulled off.

The orgasm is muffled somewhat by the circumstances but I did come and unfortunately despite her best intentions with a hanky, some of it went onto her skirt. She whispered in my ear that she needed to go to the bathroom to clean it off. The communal bathroom was across the corridor so she slipped out of the room and as the door closed Brummie let out a roar and turned to me shouting "You dirty bastard" and all I could do was roar with laughter. She certainly had her moments.

Dad had bought me a Sekonda watch for my birthday. Cost all of £4 so not exactly valuable but it was a gift from him and held great sentimental value and one day it stopped working.

It wasn't the winder-up bit, it didn't appear to be damaged (I have a poor history with smashing watches in fights or when I was drunk) but on this occasion it had just stopped. Margaret said her Dad worked in the dockyard, repairing ships meters, big clocks and such like and often repaired watches for a packet of fags. I thought it was a good offer and handed over the watch, which I never saw again.

We had a whip round one night in the Mucky Duck for another barmaid up the duff and going on what passed for maternity leave in those days. Margaret carried the pot round. At one point it contained at least one twenty-pound note, some tenner's and a lot of fivers.

We were all gobsmacked when the Landlord proudly announced we had raised over twenty-five pounds for the bulging and blushing mum to be. What happened to the rest we can only surmise that the light fingered Margaret had taken some of the notes out of it. There was a token challenge from someone who had seen them, which she denied and that was that.

Our mess lothario Rod Townend was forever berating us on our choice of squeeze for the evening. Rodders was a year or two older than the rest of us and proudly represented Hull in the dating stakes. He would aim for the more mature lady, which he always said guaranteed a shag, often all night in and occasionally a good breakfast.

We would be chasing teenage skirt that often moved faster than our hands could grab and we would return to the mess in disgrace, whilst Rods pit was usually untouched all night long as he whiled the night away in a big bed, with a woman wrapped round him and sometimes the benefit of tea and toast, or a bacon butty.

Debbie's romance with Angie took a turn for the worse when he got home from Buffers Party and found his bags packed on the maisonette landing and the door locks changed. I never quite understood why.

Her mother had a flat upstairs, so Debbie went up there to get some sympathy and a cup of tea. Well one thing led to another and so Debbie moved in with Angie's Mum for the rest of refit as she became his mature squeeze. Good on yer Dale.

We had a tough duty to undertake when six of Buffers Party were drawn to form up a firing squad for a funeral. We had to drill a few hours each day for a week and were kitted out with the trusty SLR's and a magazine of blanks each. As it was winter, we were also temporarily issued with a parade great coat, brilliant white webbing and went under the control of a gunnery petty officer.

On the day in question we jumped into a military mini bus for the round trip to Lee on Solent where the military funeral with full honours was taking place. It was a cold morning, very still and a big fog bank rolled in from the Solent which sobered up our little crew who had been cracking jokes all the way round (long way) to the cemetery.

We were stood at the back of the church during the service and then formed up to accompany the egg-crusted cortege for the burial. Firing three rounds in crisp and uniform volleys to do the guy proud.

When his wife tried to throw herself into the grave after the coffin, it set up a roll of emotion throughout those gathered including the seven of us who didn't know him. A very sad moment in time and it was a very quiet and sober mini bus that drove back round to Nelson Barracks to de-kit and hand the weapons back in to the armoury.

That pretty much completed my term in Buffers Party and I returned to chipping and painting on the mother ship until Snake Eyes called Debbie and me in for a chat in his portacabin office on the jetty.

Seems he had received a fleet wide request for a senior AB to go out to the West Coast on a big deployment on one of the Navy's glamour Type-21 frigates, HMS Ambuscade. We both wanted to go.

Snake Eyes informed us that as we each had the same seniority (day joined, date rank achieved, etc.) he couldn't separate us by the usual rules of hierarchy. Therefore, he decided that he would toss a coin to choose.

It was the only occasion I can recall when I won a toss of the coin for something so important. It happened when Debbie called heads and Snake Eyes revealed it was tails, it was off you go Perkins and pack your bags. Here is a warrant to Guzz (Devonport as we called it, Plymouth to everyone else and affectionately nicknamed Guzz by the navy).

I had one last chance for a shag with Margaret and to collect my watch from her house and I took one of my warrants to travel over to Pompey from Guzz on the first weekend I got off before we sailed. However, it was a pretty acrimonious episode when she said she wanted me to put it up her bum and I declined.

She may have been on the blob, I don't really know. Either way, there was no shag and no watch. I left and never saw her or my watch again.

Though I did hear from her, or about her one more time via correspondence... but you will have to read Book Two to find out about that

Postscript & Prologue to Book Two

In May 1978 I left HMS Antrim and was seconded to HMS Ambuscade. This first book covers my development throughout the first three and a half years in the Royal Navy, after my chequered academic experiences and time as a child and a teenager.

My second book covers the last two and a half years in the Navy and my exit into civilian life and new careers, travel and work overseas, expanding our family and continuing to enjoy life.

Opening Chapter

Born in Stockport - Grew up in the Royal Navy

HMS Ambuscade

I got the train down to Guzz and met my new shipmates the day we sailed. As I got on there was a pipe to clear lower deck and RV in the dining hall. I left my kit left with Quarter Master and I clambered down the ladders to the dining hall. I Stood at the back of the crowd whilst the Executive Officer (XO) or Number One, briefed the ships company on the forthcoming tour to an enemy port!

Shocked, as I had looked at the itinerary before I left Pompey and as far as I could see we weren't down to visit any soviet pact bases or anything similar, as the XO continued with his briefing.

The French have been our enemy since the bastards invaded us in 1066 and I don't want any of you bringing the Royal Navy into disrepute. Try keep the fighting to the back streets where you can and don't get arrested.... What an introduction.

The communicators were billeted with the chefs, stewards and storemen in 2D mess, nicknamed the Picnic Club. It didn't take long to work out why. We got all sorts of tit bits from the galley and stuff that had been destined for the wardroom but found its way down to the Picnic Club. There was always a bit of a buffet or cakes in the mess. Lovely.

Our first visit was to the French naval base at Brest. Anyone knowing their WW2 history will recall that we bombed Brest mercilessly throughout the war as it was the home to a large fleet of German submarines that were terrorising the Atlantic convoys, so desperately needed to keep the UK fed.

The fact we were there to commemorate the Battle of the Atlantic seemed somehow lost on our French hosts. It kicked off everywhere.

Printed in Poland
by Amazon Fulfillment
Poland Sp. z o.o., Wrocław

61754672R00101